EVALUATION RESEARCH AND DEVELOPMENT ACTIVITIES

Volume 68, Sage Library of Social Research

Sage Library of Social Research

Evaluation Research and Development Activities

Francis W. Hoole

Volume 68
SAGE LIBRARY OF
SOCIAL RESEARCH

 SAGE PUBLICATIONS   Beverly Hills   London

For information address:

SAGE PUBLICATIONS, INC. 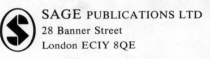 SAGE PUBLICATIONS LTD
275 South Beverly Drive   28 Banner Street
Beverly Hills, California 90212   London ECIY 8QE

Printed in the United States of America

Library of Congress Cataloging in Publication Data

Hoole, Francis W.
  Evaluation research and development activities.

  (Sage library of social research; v. 68)
  Bibliography: p. 179
  Includes index.
  1. Economic assistance—Evaluation.   2. Technical assistance—
Evaluation.   3. Evaluation research (Social action programs)
I. Title.
HC60.H667   300'.1'8   78-19842
ISBN 0-8039-1057-6
ISBN 0-8039-1058-4 pbk.

FIRST PRINTING

CONTENTS

723377

To my children
Tawny and Jonny

ACKNOWLEDGMENTS

The origins of this book can be traced to the 1974-1975 school year, which I spent in Geneva, Switzerland reading and learning from others both about evaluation research and development activities, especially by United Nations agencies. During the 1975-1976 and 1976-1977 school years I did additional reading, taught graduate and undergraduate classes on evaluation research at Indiana University, and completed a first draft of this book. The manuscript was revised extensively and sent to press during my 1977-1978 sabbatical year in Los Angeles. I owe many debts to individuals and institutions for supporting my efforts and I would like to acknowledge them.

Work on the book was facilitated by a grant from the Midwest Universities Consortium for International Activities (MUCIA) for a project on The Application of the Experimental Method to the Design and Evaluation of Technical Assistance Projects. This award was a subgrant under the United States Agency for International Development 211(d) grant AID/csd-2958 to MUCIA to finance the Program of Advanced Study in Institution Development and Technical Assistance Methodology. It was this grant that allowed me to spend the 1974-1975 academic year in Geneva doing research. The Carnegie Endowment for International Peace and the Centre de Recherches sur les Institutions Internationales facilitated work on the project by providing office space and secretarial assistance in Geneva during the 1974-1975 period. The International Development Institute at Indiana University provided valuable office space and secretarial aid during the spring of 1974 as I was preparing to go to Geneva. The Political Science Department at Indiana University has provided office space and secretarial assistance for me ever since I joined its faculty in 1970, and its assistance on this project was especially valuable during the 1975-1977 period. The Institute for Marine and Coastal Studies at the University of Southern California provided an office and secretarial assistance during the 1977-1978 period. A 1976 summer faculty fellowship from Indiana University and a 1977-1978 sabbatical year grant from Indiana University provided valuable time for writing.

I am grateful to the University of Wisconsin Press for permission to use material throughout the book which originally appeared in Francis W. Hoole, "Evaluating the Impact of International Organizations," *International Organization* 31, 3:541-563 (copyright 1977 by the Regents of the University of Wisconsin). I am grateful to the Wayne State University Press and to my coauthors for permission to use material in Chapter 6 of this book which originally appeared in Francis W. Hoole, Brian L. Job, and Harvey J. Tucker, "Incremental Budgeting and International Organizations," *American Journal of Political Science* 20, 2:273-301 (copyright 1976 by the Wayne State University Press). I am grateful to the Indiana University Press for permission to use material in Chapter 6 of this book which originally appeared in Francis W. Hoole, *Politics and Budgeting in the World Health Organization* (Bloomington, Indiana: copyright 1976 by Indiana University Press).

I am especially grateful to the following individuals for providing guidance, suggestions, encouragement, and assistance on the project: Ron Anderson, Robert Boruch, Robert Bowen, Donald Campbell, James Caporaso, Remi Clignet, Charles Cnudde, Jacques Copland, Brian Flay, John Fobes, Robert Friedheim, John Goormaghtigh, Jeff Green, David Handley, Brian Job, John McDonald, Charles Ostrom, Alice Rivlin, Wolf Scott, Feliciano Sicat, Milton Siegel, William Siffin, Jean Siotis, Grafton Trout, Harvey Tucker, and Ned Wallace. I owe a special debt to Patrick McGowan for spending many hours suggesting and discussing improvements as I worked on the final draft. Lars Jensen greatly improved the final product through his editing and handling of the manuscript for Sage Publications. My wife Leanne, daughter Tanya, and son Jonathan supported and encouraged me in every way.

I gratefully acknowledge the support which I have received on this project. Without it the book would not have been possible. Naturally the final product and any errors contained in it are my responsibility.

Francis W. Hoole
Los Angeles, California
March, 1978

INTRODUCTION

In recent years the government of the United States has pursued a foreign aid strategy in the agricultural field which emphasizes the goals of increasing income and production of peasant farmers in developing countries. In line with this strategy, a rural sector loan of twenty-three million dollars to the government of Guatemala was approved in February of 1970 by the Agency for International Development of the U.S. government.[1] Most of the money provided by the loan was earmarked for agricultural credit and technical assistance activities. The major goals of the loan were "to increase basic food grain production and income among small farmers in the [Guatemalan] Highlands."[2]

How successful in meeting these goals were the Guatemalan activities supported by the loan? Does the U.S. foreign aid strategy in the agricultural field seem to be working? Unfortunately it is not possible to give reliable answers which are based on the experience with the 1970 rural sector loan to Guatemala. The activities financed by the loan were part of a Guatemalan rural development plan which included several different programs. And as John R. Davidson has noted, "little data exist measuring the impact of these programs."[3]

The Agency for International Development did conduct two different studies which attempted to assess the effectiveness of the activities financed by the 1970 Guatemalan loan. The first study found that (1) "Credit-using farms employed 20-40% more labor than non-credit using farms";[4] (2) "the value of . . . [credit-using farms] production averaged 32% more than that found on non-credit farms";[5] and (3) "net income on credit-using farms averaged 63% higher than on non-credit farms."[6] The second study found that "no consistent conclusions can be drawn regarding the income and production differences associated with the use of credit and . . . the generalized conclusions . . . [from the first study] are misleading."[7]

How are we to decide what was the impact of the loan? Unfortunately there is no real basis for making a decision. The lessons from the 1970 U.S. rural sector loan of twenty-three million dollars to the Guatemalan government are not clear because no reliable evaluation was conducted of the impact of the activities financed by the loan.

Even more unfortunate is the fact that frequently there is no solid basis for knowing what impact development activities have had, and this is true of subnational, national, bilateral, and multilateral development activities. This book was written because I believe, for both policy and theory building reasons, that we need to understand better the impact of activities designed to bring about political, economic, and social development, however defined.

"So What" Questions

What difference do development activities make? This question and its various versions concerning impacts, effectiveness, goal achievement, and side effects form a set of important questions which I will call "so what" questions.

Only a decade ago these questions were of interest primarily from an academic standpoint. Those most frequently asking the questions were scholars who were working on theories of the development process. However little more of a systematic nature is known today about the effects of development activities than was known ten years ago.

"So what" questions also have significant practical importance as it becomes increasingly apparent that numerous development programs of national governments are ineffective and as various technical assistance agencies undergo crises concerning their abilities to accomplish objectives. Development problems are more complex than was once thought, and theories and strategies for development seem less helpful for designing programs and activities than they appeared to be a decade ago. There is a growing realization that we do not understand how to bring about social, economic, and political development, however defined. There are widespread feelings that we do not know what works, that it is essential that better knowledge be generated regarding development strategies, and that better information be made available for decisions on the allocation of scarce resources for development. This has resulted in an interest on the part of policy-makers in learning from development activities by setting them up in such a way that they can be evaluated systematically. There is an interest in determining which aspects of development activities are effective and which are not, and in using this information to make modifications in the activities.[8]

The age of governmental accountability is also upon us. As Edward A. Suchman has noted, "social institutions, whether medical, educational, religious, economic, or political, are required to provide 'proof' of their legitimacy and effectiveness in order to justify society's continued support."[9] Although accountability concerns may vary greatly according to nation and organization, many agencies working in the development field are being asked to justify continued financial support, to demonstrate that they have accomplished something, and to show that their activities have made a difference. There is also an interest in "so what" questions on the part of those to whom development policy-makers are responsible, especially those paying for the activities.

However, these concerns are not unique to the development field. "So what" questions also have been directed toward activities in the public sector in developed countries. A considerable body of literature has recently appeared in the United States on the use of systematic evaluation techniques to provide evidence on the effectiveness of social action programs. This literature contains an approach that is of relevance for obtaining reliable answers to "so what" questions in the development field. It calls for a hard-nosed look at whether a social action program has had an impact and forms the basis for what has come to be known as the evaluation research movement.

The Evaluation Research Movement

As we know it today, the evaluation research movement is about a decade old. It is based primarily in the United States, and among those involved are political scientists, sociologists, psychologists, educators, medical doctors, agricultural specialists, economists, anthropologists, lawyers, statisticians, and operations researchers, as well as legislators and bureaucrats. The results of evaluation research studies have been published in disciplinary periodicals and numerous books as well as in two new journals, *Evaluation* and *Evaluation Quarterly,* which deal exclusively with evaluation research matters. There is also a new yearbook, *Evaluation Studies Review Annual,*[10] and in 1975 a *Handbook of Evaluation Research*[11] was published. The movement is held together by an Evaluation Research Society, which was founded in 1976.

Among the indicators of growing interest in evaluation research in the United States are the following: (1) the Social Science Research Council recently completed a major project which brought together leading American experts on evaluation research and produced a state of the art book;[12] (2) the National Science Foundation recently emphasized funding for evaluation research; (3) graduate and undergraduate courses on the topic are being offered at some universities; (4) there is a growing number of jobs in evaluation research at the federal, state, and local government levels; and (5) evaluation research panels were organized at the 1976 American Society for Public Administration meetings. Recently, such agencies as the World Bank, the International Labor Organization, the World Health Organization, the United States Agency for International Development, and the United Nations Educational, Scientific, and Cultural Organization have undertaken special studies on evaluation research in the development field.

Throughout the world, more than one hundred fifty social experiments have been undertaken to evaluate the impact of social action programs,[13] and numerous quasi-experimental and correlational studies have been conducted with the same goal in mind. These evaluations have taken place in a number of fields, such as health, agriculture, and education. Perhaps the most famous evaluation research studies have dealt with income maintenance and head start programs in the United States, the Sesame Street educational television program in Mexico, the family planning program in Taiwan, and the use of breathalysers in a program to deter drunk driving in the United Kingdom.[14]

A basic bibliography of evaluation research would include several hundred items, most of which are addressed primarily to domestic concerns in developed countries. Because there are already several good overviews of the evaluation research literature, there is no need to review it here in detail.[15] Some general comments are in order so that the essence of the evaluation research approach will be clarified for the reader and the discussion of its potential utility in the development field will be facilitated.

The Evaluation Research Approach

Within the evaluation research movement there is no commonly accepted definition of the concept of evaluation. However, most evaluation researchers would not disagree too much with Suchman's view of evaluation as "the determination (whether based on opinions, records, subjective or objective data) of the results (whether desirable or undesirable; transient or permanent; immediate or delayed) attained by some activity (whether a program, or part of a program, a drug or a therapy, an ongoing or one shot approach) designed to accomplish some valued goal or objective (whether ultimate, intermediate, or immediate, effort or performance, long or short range)."[16] There also would be considerable agreement with Joseph S. Wholey and his associates when they contend that "evaluation is research, the application of the scientific method to experience with public programs to learn what happens as a result of program activities."[17]

The evaluation research approach can be seen as one of several quantitative approaches of potential relevance for the evaluation of public policies. Its orientation toward evaluation is different from, but complements, that of several other public policy analysis techniques. It can be distinguished from optimization techniques, such as linear programming, which focus primarily on evaluating possible alternatives and determining the optimal mix regarding the allocation of resources, given an objective function and a certain set of constraints. It can be distinguished from the orientation toward evaluation of systematic monitoring methods, such as network analysis, as well as traditional audit reports and financial statements, which focus primarily on the process by which a program is implemented. The evaluation research approach is also different from that employed in cost-benefit and cost-effectiveness techniques, which emphasize the evaluation of efficiency, and that utilized in many planning and forecasting techniques, which try to evaluate the future through the extension of past trends. The main concern of the evaluation research methodology is obtaining objective empirical evidence regarding the actual effectiveness of social action programs. The evidence can be used as the basis for optimization, cost-benefit, and other analyses, or simply as general information for policy-makers, those to whom policy-makers are responsible (e.g., citizens), and scholars.

The evaluation research approach toward evaluating impacts differs from, and complements, that found in the normal environmental impact statement. Whereas environmental impact statements usually try to estimate what the impact will be, evaluation research attempts to determine what the impact actually was. Furthermore, the evaluation research approach usually focuses on a variety of impacts beyond, but sometimes including, environmental concerns. The evaluation research methodology could be used to evaluate whether the projections of environmental impact statements turned out to be correct.

Evaluation research is concerned with the full range of operational procedures involved in the systematic empirical examination of hypotheses regarding the impact of a social action program. A falsification strategy is followed in the testing of impact hypotheses. Correlation is carefully distinguished from causation, and a systematic effort to disconfirm the obtained results (not just empirically supported impact hypotheses) is required through the examination of plausible rival explanations. The work of psychologist Donald T. Campbell and his associates provides the basic methodological orientation for evaluation research.[18] Campbell and his associates have presented approximately twenty different experimental, quasi-experimental, and preexperimental research designs that are useful in various circumstances for controlling plausible rival hypotheses and evaluating the impact of social action programs.

The key ingredient in evaluation research is the use of the scientific method to test hypotheses concerning the impact of social action programs.[19] Evaluation research is not mechanical and does not dictate which variables to include or exclude in an analysis, how to measure concepts or operationalize variables, or which impact hypotheses to test. It emphasizes flexibility in obtaining knowledge and urges the researcher to use the scientific method and to examine cause and effect statements about the impact of social action programs. The potential relevance of this approach for the examination of "so what" questions in the development field is obvious.

The Potential Uses of Evaluation Research

Evaluation research can be used when two conditions exist: (1) there is a clearly stated hypothesis regarding the impact of a social action program; and (2) it is possible to obtain relevant and reliable data for the specified variables. The validity and reliability of the evaluation research study however will depend on a number of factors, such as the quality of data and research design and the care exercised by the researchers in employing various research techniques. Whether any given study is substantively meaningful is something to be determined by those planning the study and using the results.

There appear to be three different groups who might benefit from the use of evaluation research in studying development activities. Scholars might use it to "add to knowledge available about social and interpersonal behavior and the social environment, and to explicate and refine the practice principles that underlie programming efforts."[20] Policy-makers might use it to generate knowledge on policy, program, and project effectiveness that can be used as feedback information to assist in the making of decisions regarding possible social programs. Evaluation research can also be used to supply information needed for holding policy-makers accountable for their organization's actions. This latter use would be of greatest interest to those to whom policy-makers are responsible, such as taxpayers and legislators.

Evaluation research is potentially relevant for the examination of a wide range of development issues, such as health, education, agriculture, and family planning. It would be helpful in the study of the impact of policy changes, projects, programs, program strategies, laws, court decisions, changes in institutional arrangements, funding levels, leadership styles, and other similar activities. Because of complexity and cost evaluation research should not be used to examine questions when the answer is already well known and accepted without controversy or to examine trivial questions.

In many studies the essential concern will be whether a specific development activity has been effective. The evaluation research approach is appropriate for this type of concern. For many development specialists, however, the crucial question will be: how effective is a specific development activity in relation to other possible ways of attacking a problem? By allowing for the expansion of the basic research design to include more than one type of social action program and by treating the cases without the development activity as control group cases, evaluation research facilitates this type of inquiry.

For some development specialists the problems that are most significant, and at the same time most interesting, concern what might be labeled indirect impact. The effect might take place in a complex system of interaction in which important consequences are latent rather than manifest. The initial problem is to define the nature of the impact, including possible latent as well as manifest consequences. The evaluation research approach offers no dogmatic or magic solution to these specification and measurement problems. It encourages initiative and creativity in identifying and measuring impact variables, whether latent or manifest, goal-derived or un-anticipated.

This book will attempt to clarify what evaluation research is. In addition, it will suggest specific situations where it is promising to utilize the approach to study the impact of development activities. The existing evaluation research literature has focused primarily on the American context and a separate statement for the development field is required. This field is complex and no simple guidelines can be offered regarding when to raise "so what" questions and when to undertake studies. The feasibility and worth of each potential study will need to be examined in light of its specific circumstances, and there can be no substitute for the insights and judgments on this matter by knowledgable development specialists.

An Orienting Perspective

This book presents the prospects and problems in utilizing the evaluation research approach in the development context. It contains an introduction to the evaluation research movement and approach, an overview of the methodology of evaluation research, case studies which demonstrate the use of different evaluation research designs, discussions of applied research problems and research utilization problems likely to be encountered in the development context, and conclusions, implications, and suggestions for research. The bibliography presents the basic evaluation research publications. The book is intended primarily for development specialists, both practitioners and scholars, who desire an overview of evaluation research but do not want to read a long methodologically oriented book on the topic. It assumes no knowledge of evaluation research.

Many individuals in the evaluation research movement make a distinction between formative and summative evaluation.[21] Formative evaluation means examining an activity while it is under way and summative evaluation focuses upon it after its completion. Formative evaluation is of interest in most circumstances. For example, knowledge on the effectiveness of activities which is uncovered during the implementation of an annual program may provide useful information to policy-makers responsible for adjustments to the following year's program, to scholars testing hypotheses of theoretical interest, and to citizens that are paying taxes to support the activity. Summative evaluation, on the other hand, will be useful when information can reasonably be utilized after the completion of specific program activities. This latter type of information may be quite helpful to policy-makers in convincing others of the value of a specific agency or a certain type of program and in determining what type of institutional arrangements or program worked, or to scholars testing hypotheses of theoretical interest. Whereas there are differences of degree in doing and utilizing information from formative and summative evaluations, at the most general level they are not crucial, and they will not be emphasized in this book. Both formative and summative evaluation studies focus on the impact of social action programs and are based on the same methodological orientation, although differences in timing may mean that greater care is taken and that different designs and techniques are used in some circumstances.

Some people have made a distinction between impact and process evaluation.[22] The essential idea of process evaluation is that the independent variable (usually a program, project or strategy) in the hypothesis regarding the impact of a social action program should be examined carefully. However, there does not appear to be any distinctive or unique methodology that has been advanced for process evaluation, and at times it seems that the concern is with traditional management matters. In this book the careful examination of the independent variable in an impact hypothesis will be emphasized, and the management of the implementation of social action programs will be discussed, but no special discussion will be provided of process evaluation per se. Some readers may want to consult the relevant literature on this topic.

Other people in the evaluation research movement have suggested a switch from a paradigm that emphasizes objectivity and the testing of impact hypotheses to one that emphasizes subjective probability estimates of likely outcomes of social action programs and the integration of these estimates into the policy-making process through use of a decision-theoretic approach employing bayesian statistics and multi-attribute utility analysis.[23] The primary basis of this critique of the impact hypothesis orientation relates to research utilization problems. In Chapter 6 I will treat the bayesian decision techniques as being potentially complementary to the evaluation research approach, but the details of the bayesian methodology will not be presented. The interested reader may want to consult the relevant literature.

The Remaining Chapters

Chapter 1 presents the basic methodology of evaluation research. Special attention is given to impact hypotheses, plausible rival hypotheses, evaluation research designs, measurement concerns, data collection procedures, and data analysis techniques. No detailed discussion of methodological techniques is offered. The use of a certain amount of jargon is necessary, but an effort is made to keep it to a minimum.

The major contribution of the evaluation research methodology is that it makes possible more reliable causal inferences regarding the impact of social action programs by controlling rival explanations of observed results. A report is presented in Chapter 2 on the smallpox eradication program of the World Health Organization (WHO). That program, in turn, serves as the basis for a demonstration of the use of the evaluation research methodology in the development field. The smallpox study demonstrates how the evaluation research methodology can be of assistance in ruling out rival explanations of the impact of development activities through the use of time-series data. The quasi-experimental design that is featured is the most powerful design possible when time-series data are available but control group data cannot be used.

When control group cases are employed but have not been identified through the use of randomization they are called nonequivalent control group cases. One of the most powerful means of controlling rival explanations of the impact of social action programs involves the use of nonequivalent control group data. In fact, several quasi-experimental designs are based upon that strategy. In order to demonstrate the use of nonequivalent control group data, a case study is offered in Chapter 3 of the Indonesian green revolution rice program, and rice programs in Burma and Thailand are used as nonequivalent control group cases. The evaluation research design that is featured in Chapter 3 combines the use of time-series data and nonequivalent control group data and is, generally speaking, the most powerful quasi-experimental design available to evaluation researchers.

The principal advantage of experimental research designs is that they equate treatment and control groups through randomization, thereby isolating the effect of the treatment and ruling out numerous rival explanations. A report on the evaluation of Plaza Sesamo in Mexico is presented in Chapter 4 in order to provide an illustration of the use of the classical experiment in the development field.

The most serious difficulties in utilizing the evaluation research methodology in the development field will be of an applied nature, although the seriousness of these problems will vary from study to study. A discussion of applied research problems that are likely to be encountered by development specialists is presented in Chapter 5. Special attention is given to problems of impact hypotheses, measurement concerns, data collection procedures, data analysis techniques, ethical concerns, organizational factors, and evaluation research designs. The uniqueness of applied research problems in the development field is also discussed.

There are potentially serious problems in the use of evaluation research conclusions by policy-makers, with timing and relevance of the findings being the most serious concerns. A general discussion of research utilization problems is presented in Chapter 6, where an attempt is made to identify those problems likely to be faced by policy-makers in the development field. The discussion is oriented around the policy-making process because development activities are the result of an inherently political process. If the evaluation research approach is to be an aid to decision-making, it must be useful in the policy-making process. An attempt is made to give the research utilization discussion substantive meaning by focusing on the budgetary process of the World Health Organization. It is shown how an evaluation research subsystem might be added to the WHO budgetary process and a presentation follows of how the evaluation research approach complements several other quantitative public policy analysis techniques. A discussion is presented of how the research utilization problems might be different in other agencies in the development field and in nonbudgetary processes.

Chapter 7 is devoted to summarizing conclusions, implications, and suggestions for research.

NOTES

1. For information regarding this loan, see John R. Davidson, "AID rural development strategy in Guatemala: mechanisms for reaching the small farmer and their impact," paper prepared for presentation at the seventh national meeting of the Latin American Studies Association, November 13, 1977, Houston, Texas. I would like to thank Patrick J. McGowan for calling this paper to my attention and suggesting that material from it be used in this chapter.

2. Davidson, op. cit.: 12.

3. Davidson, op. cit.: 17.

4. Davidson, op. cit.: 17.

5. Davidson, op. cit.: 17.

6. Davidson, op. cit.: 18.

7. Davidson, op. cit.: 18.

8. Alice M. Rivlin has influenced this thinking by arguing convincingly when discussing social action programs: "Until programs are organized so that analysts can learn from them and systematic experimentation is undertaken on a significant scale, prospects seem dim for learning how to produce better social services." Alice M. Rivlin, *Systematic Thinking for Social Action* (Washington, D.C.: Brookings Institution, 1971): 64.

9. Edward A. Suchman, *Evaluative Research: Principles and Practice in Public Service and Social Action Programs* (New York: Russell Sage, 1967): 2.

10. *Evaluation Studies Review Annual* (Beverly Hills: Sage Publications, annually starting in 1976).

11. Elmer L. Struening and Marcia Guttentag, eds., *Handbook of Evaluation Research,* Volume 1 (Beverly Hills: Sage Publications, 1975); and Marcia Guttentag and Elmer L. Struening, eds., *Handbook of Evaluation Research,* Volume 2 (Beverly Hills: Sage Publications, 1975).

12. Henry Riecken, Robert F. Boruch, Donald T. Campbell, Nathan Caplan, Thomas K. Glennan, Jr., John W. Pratt, Albert Rees, and Walter Williams, *Social Experimentation: A Method For Planning Social Intervention* (New York: Academic Press, 1974).

13. Robert F. Boruch, "Bibliography: illustrative randomized field experiments for planning and evaluation," mimeo, Evanston, Illinois, Northwestern University, 1974.

14. Cf., David N. Kershaw, "The New Jersey negative income tax experiment: a summary of the design, operations and results of the first large-scale social science experiment," in Gene M. Lyons, ed., *Social Research and Public Policies: The Dartmouth/OECD Conference* (Hanover, N.H.: University Press of New England, 1975): 87-116; Victor Cicarelli, "The inpact of Head Start: executive summary," in *The Impact of Head Start: An Evaluation of the Effects of Head Start on Children's Cognitive and Affective Development,* Volume 1 (Bladensburg, Maryland: Westinghouse Learning Corporation, 1969): 1-11; Rogelio Diaz-Guerrero and Wayne H. Holtzman, "Learning by televised 'Plaza Sesamo' in Mexico," *Journal of Educational Psychology* 66 (1974): 632-43; Ronald Freedman and John Y. Takeshita, *Family Planning in Taiwan: An Experiment in Social Change* (Princeton, N.J.: Princeton University Press, 1969); and H. Laurence Ross, Donald T. Campbell, and Gene V. Glass, "Determining the social effects of a legal reform: the British 'Breathalyser' crackdown of 1967," *American Behavioral Scientist* 13 (1970): 493-509.

15. Cf., Carol H. Weiss, *Evaluation Research: Methods of Assessing Effectiveness* (Englewood Cliffs, N.J.: Prentice-Hall, 1972); Riecken et al., *Social Experimentation;* Joseph S. Wholey, John W. Scanlon, Hugh G. Duffy, James S. Fukumoto, and Leona M. Vogt, *Federal Evaluation Policy: Analyzing The Effects of Public Programs* (Washington, D.C.: Urban Institute, 1973); Rivlin, *Systematic Thinking for Social Action;* Samuel P. Hayes, Jr., *Evaluating Development Projects* (Paris: United Nations Educational, Scientific and Cultural Organization, 1966); Howard E. Freeman and Clarence C. Sherwood, *Social Research and Social Policy* (Englewood Cliffs, N.J.: Prentice-Hall, 1970); Ilene N. Bernstein and Howard E. Freeman, *Academic and Entrepreneurial Research: The Consequences of Diversity in Federal Evaluation Studies* (New York: Russell Sage, 1975); Agency for International Development, *Evaluation Handbook* (Washington, D.C.: Agency for International Development, 1974); Francis G. Caro, ed., *Readings in Evaluation Research* (New York: Russell Sage, 1971); Lyons, ed., *Social Research and Public Policies;* Peter H. Rossi and Walter Williams, eds., *Evaluating Social Programs: Theory, Practice and Politics* (New York: Seminar Press, 1972); Carol H. Weiss, ed., *Evaluating Action Programs: Readings in Social Action and Education* (Boston: Allyn and Bacon, 1972); Struening and Guttentag, eds., *Handbook of Evaluation Research;* Guttentag and Struening, eds., *Handbook of Evaluation Research;* Suchman, *Evaluative Research;* and, Howard E. Freeman, "The present status of evaluation research," in Marcia Guttentag with Shalom Saar, eds., *Evaluation Studies Review Annual,* Volume 2 (Beverly Hills: Sage Publications, 1977): 17-51.

16. Suchman, *Evaluative Research:* 31-2.

17. Wholey et al., *Federal Evaluation Policy:* 19.

18. The basic works are Donald T. Campbell and Julian C. Stanley, *Experimental and Quasi-Experimental Designs for Research* (Chicago: Rand McNally, 1963); Donald T. Campbell, "Reforms as experiments," *American Psychologist* 24 (1969): 409-429; Donald T. Campbell and H. Laurence Ross, "The Connecticut crackdown on speeding: time series data in quasi-experimental analysis," *Law and Society Review* 3 (1968): 33-53; Ross, Campbell, and Glass, "Determining the social effects of a legal reform"; Riecken et al., *Social Experimentation;* Donald T. Campbell, "Assessing the impact of planned social change," in Lyons, ed., *Social Research and Public Policies: 3-45;* Thomas D. Cook and Donald T. Campbell, "The design and conduct of quasi-experiments and true experiments in field settings," in M.D. Dunnette, ed., *Handbook of Industrial and Organizational Research* (Chicago: Rand McNally, 1976): 223-326; and Donald T. Campbell and Robert F. Boruch, "Making the case for randomized

assignment to treatments by considering the alternatives: six ways in which quasi-experimental evaluations in compensatory education tend to underestimate effects," in Carl A. Bennett and Arthur A. Lumsdaine, eds., *Evaluation and Experiment: Some Critical Issues in Assessing Social Programs* (New York: Academic Press, 1975): 195-296.

19. For an introduction to the scientific method, see Morris R. Cohen and Ernest Nagel, *An Introduction to Logic and Scientific Method* (New York: Harcourt, Brace and Company, 1934); and Richard S. Rudner, *Philosophy of Social Science* (Englewood Cliffs, N.J.: Prentice-Hall, 1966).

20. Bernstein and Freeman, *Academic and Entrepreneurial Research:* 1.

21. Many publications contain discussions of formative and summative evaluation. For an introduction, see Michael Scriven, "The methodology of evaluation," in Weiss, ed., *Evaluating Action Programs:* 123-136.

22. Cf., Berstein and Freeman, *Academic and Entrepreneurial Research:* 18-19, 65-82; and Freeman, "The present status of evaluation research ": 25-26, 30-39.

23. Ward Edwards, Marcia Guttentag, and Kurt Snapper, "A decision-theoretic approach to evaluation research," in Struening and Guttentag, eds., *Handbook of Evaluation Research:* 139-181; Marcia Guttentag, "An approach to evaluation," unpublished paper SHC.75/WS/3, United Nations Educational, Scientific and Cultural Organization, Paris, 3 February, 1975; Marcia Guttentag, "Subjectivity and its use in evaluation research," *Evaluation* 1 (1973): 60-65; Marcia Guttentag, "Evaluation of social intervention programs," *Annals of the New York Academy of Sciences* 218 (1973): 3-13; Marcia Guttentag and Kurt Snapper, "Plans, evaluations, and decisions," *Evaluation* 2 (1974): 58-64, 73-74; Ward Edwards and Marcia Guttentag, "Experiments and evaluations: a reexamination," in Bennett and Lumsdaine, eds., *Evaluation and Experiment:* 409-63; and Marcia Guttentag, "Evaluation and society," *Personality and Social Psychology* 3 (1977): 31-40.

Chapter 1

THE METHODOLOGY OF EVALUATION RESEARCH

If empirical evidence is used to evaluate the impact of social action programs, then the means by which that evidence is gathered, assigned values, and analyzed are extremely important. The evaluation research methodology is accordingly focused on just those matters. It is concerned with the full range of operational procedures involved in the systematic empirical examination of hypotheses regarding the impact of social action programs. The evaluation research methodology can be seen as the extension to policy-related questions of certain aspects of the behavioral science methodology which has been so popular in the social sciences in America during the last few years.

It is the hypothesis (defined as a "conjectural statement of the relation between two or more variables"[1]) that sets up the empirical examination in an evaluation research study. Both impact hypotheses and plausible rival hypotheses are of importance in the evaluation research methodology, and they will be discussed initially. The research design establishes the plan for the examination of impact hypotheses and the control of plausible rival hypotheses. Several of the more relevant evaluation research designs for the development field are presented next. Measurement concerns, data collection procedures, and data analysis techniques are then discussed.

Impact Hypotheses

The impact hypothesis suggests that there is a relationship between the social action program, or some aspect of it, and a measure or indicator of some behavior or condition. An example of an impact hypothesis will be found in the smallpox eradication program case study in Chapter 2. It sets up the reported empirical examination and is stated in the following manner: The intensified worldwide smallpox eradication program of the World Health Organization resulted in a reduction in the number of countries in the world reporting cases of smallpox.

Several things should be noted about the impact hypothesis: The independent variable may be the entire social action program or any aspect of it, such as a program strategy or an alternative means of implementing a project. Thus, the focus may be on the project, program, or any other meaningful unit of analysis. The dependent (impact) variable may be an indicator of a goal or a side effect. In most instances an investigator will examine several independent and dependent variables. A comprehensive evaluation of a development activity would undoubtedly involve numerous important issues, and hence studies utilizing multiple impact hypotheses are to be encouraged.

Great care must be taken to select impact hypotheses which lead to meaningful evaluation research studies. The evaluation research methodology offers no help in the important task of identifying the appropriate variables and the character of the relationship between them. In some situations the impact hypotheses may be derived formally from an axiomatic theory. Yet, in most instances the impact hypotheses will be of an ad hoc nature and will be based on the circumstances surrounding a specific activity and the insights and interests of those specifying the hypotheses. The same methodological approach is used to test derived and ad hoc hypotheses.

At the heart of the evaluation research methodology is the idea that it is impossible to prove that the social action program caused an observed change in the impact variable. Hence the causal explanation contained in an impact hypothesis is retained (is not rejected) only if three conditions are met: (1) the cause preceded the effect in time; (2) treatments covary with effects (if the cause and effect are not related, then one could not cause the other); and (3) there are no alternative explanations that are more plausible. The plausible rival hypotheses deal with all three of these matters, providing criteria for infering causality. The strongest possible causal interpretation for an impact hypothesis is when there is strong empirical support for it and an apparent refutation of all plausible rival hypotheses.

Plausible Rival Hypotheses

In any test of an impact hypothesis there will be alternative explanations for the results that are observed.[2] Many of these explanations form the basis for rival hypotheses that utilize the same dependent variable as the impact hypothesis but employ alternative independent variables. Other explanations suggest why no impact was observed. Examples of rival explanations will be found in the following chapters. In the smallpox eradication program case study one plausible rival hypothesis takes the following form: Specific events occurring at the same time as the intensified worldwide smallpox eradication program of the World Health Organization resulted in a reduction in the number of countries in the world reporting cases of smallpox. In this statement a new independent variable has been substituted for the original one in the impact hypothesis.

Thomas D. Cook and Donald T. Campbell have identified thirty-five potential rival explanations.[3] They have classified them into four categories: (1) internal validity; (2) statistical conclusion validity; (3) external validity; and (4) construct validity. Internal validity is most important and "the priority-ordering of the other . . . [types of validity] varies with the kind of research being conducted."[4]

The threat to internal validity casts doubt on whether the hypothesized causal relationship between operational versions of the variables specified in the impact hypothesis actually exists in the specific circumstances that are examined. There are fourteen challenges to internal validity.

History. Specific events occurring at the same time as the activity being evaluated might account for the observed impact.

Maturation. The maturation explanation suggests that "processes within the respondents or observed social units producing changes [in the impact variable] as a function of the passage of time per se, such as growth, fatigue, [or] secular trends"[5] might have caused the observed impact.

Testing. The effect of earlier tests upon the scores obtained on later tests of the impact variable might have produced the observed impact.

Instrumentation. The observed impact may be due to a change in the means of measuring the impact variable.

Statistical regression. This explanation is concerned with a possible statistical artifact: "If the group was selected because it was extreme on some measure [of the impact variable], statistical reasoning indicates that it will appear less extreme on subsequent tests [of the impact variable], even though the intervening treatment may be completely ineffectual."[6]

Selection. The differential selection of cases for treatment and control groups may have produced the observed difference between groups.

Mortality. The differential loss of cases for treatment and control groups may have produced the observed difference between groups.

Interactions with selection. One or several of the aforementioned explanations might have interacted with selection to produce the observed impact.

Ambiguity about the direction of causal inference. It may not be possible to tell which variable is actually the cause and which is the effect. This explanation is a threat especially when a cross-sectional correlational study is undertaken.

Diffusion or imitation of the treatment. The cases in the control group may have received the treatment through diffusion or imitation and thus the treatment may have been eliminated as a possible cause of the difference in impact observed for the groups.

Compensatory equalization of treatment. The treatment may have been given to both the treatment and control groups, thereby eliminating the treatment as a possible cause for the difference in impact observed for the groups.

Compensatory rivalry. A competitive spirit may have developed in the control group and motivated an effort which clouds the real difference between it and the treatment group on the impact variable.

Resentful demoralization of respondents receiving less desirable treatments. The respondents in the control group may have become resentful and demoralized because they did not receive the treatment. They may have acted in such a way that created a bias in the observed results.

Local history. The "different treatments . . . [may] be associated with all the unique historical experiences that each group has"[7] and the treatment may not be responsible for the observed difference between groups.

The rival explanations in the internal validity category are the most important because they raise questions about whether the obtained results can be interpreted causally.

Statistical conclusion validity is concerned with whether the conclusion regarding the impact was a statistical artifact resulting from inappropriate uses of statistical techniques. There are six explanations in this category.

Statistical power. The statistical techniques that were used may have led to an incorrect conclusion because of small sample size, an inappropriate setting of the level of significance, or the selection of a one-sided hypothesis.

Fishing and the error rate problem. Chance might have produced the statistical conclusion regarding impact. This explanation is a threat especially when a search involving a large number of differences is undertaken.

The reliability of measures. Measures of low reliability may have produced the statistical conclusion regarding impact.

The reliability of treatment implementation. Lack of standardization of the implementation of the social action program may have produced the statistical conclusion regarding impact.

Random irrelevancies in the experimental setting. Features of the experimental setting other than the treatment may have produced the statistical conclusion regarding impact.

Random heterogeneity of respondents. Heterogeneity of respondents with respect to variables that affect the impact variable may have produced the statistical conclusion regarding impact.

These explanations cast doubt on the test of the null hypothesis regarding impact and therefore on the conclusions arrived at through the use of statistics.

External validity focuses on whether the observed results of an impact study can be expected to be the same at a later time, such as next year, in a different setting, such as another country, or when other persons are involved. This category contains six explanations.

Interaction of treatments and treatments. It may not be valid to generalize to a situation where only one treatment is given if the cases in the treatment group received more than one treatment.

Interaction of testing and treatment. It may not be valid to generalize to situations where the testing is not identical.

Interaction of selection and treatment. It may not be valid to generalize to situations where the categories of respondents are not identical.

Interaction of setting and treatment. It may not be valid to generalize to situations where the setting is not identical.

Interaction of history and treatment. It may not be valid to generalize to situations in the past and future because they are not identical.

Generalizing across effect constructs. The observed impact might not hold for other impact variables and constructs.

These confounding explanations are relevant only when an attempt is made to generalize to other times, settings, and persons.

The rival explanations that focus on problems of generalization from operational measures to theoretical constructs are in the construct validity category. There are nine explanations of this type.

Inadequate preoperational explication of constructs. Inadequate initial clarification of the theoretical construct may have led to the development of operational measures which do not adequately represent the construct.

Mono-operation bias. Single operational measures may underrepresent a construct and/or contain irrelevancies.

Mono-method bias. The use of the same method for giving treatments and/or collecting data on responses may result in a bias in regard to the construct.

Hypothesis-guessing within experimental conditions. The subjects may have tried to guess the hypothesis being tested and the observed impact may have been generated as a reaction to that guess.

Evaluation apprehension. The subjects may be apprehensive about being evaluated and therefore may have biased their reported attitudes or behavior.

Experimenter expectancies. The observed impact may have been the result of a data collection bias resulting from the hopes and expectations of the experimenter.

Confounding levels of constructs and constructs. The operational procedures may not have covered the full range of possible values for the variables and thus may have missed part of the relationship between variables.

Generalizing across time. It may not be valid to generalize from the impact observed using the operational measures to the conclusion that the impact would hold across time for the theoretical construct because the observed impact may be of a short duration.

Interaction of procedure and treatment. The operational procedures may have allowed the respondents to gain information which created a bias in the observed results.

These confounding explanations are of interest only when an attempt is made to generalize across treatments and measures to theoretical constructs.

The evaluation research approach follows a falsification strategy in testing impact hypotheses. Correlation is distinguished carefully from causation and a systematic effort to disconfirm observed impact results is required through the examination of each of the rival explanations. The listing of challenges to the validity of impact studies may seem so overwhelming that some individuals might want to forgo undertaking such studies. This is not a satisfactory alternative because rival explanations do exist and they present challenges to the causal explanation contained in any study, although different rival hypotheses may be relevant in different studies. The evaluation research approach attempts to make explicit the rival explanations and to control them through the use of the evaluation research design.

Evaluation Research Designs

Campbell and his associates have presented over twenty different basic research designs that are useful in various circumstances for controlling explanations in the internal validity category.[8] These basic designs are of three types: (1) experimental; (2) quasi-experimental; and (3) preexperimental.[9] They control rival explanations in the internal validity category and provide the primary basis for evaluation research studies.

The methods of controlling explanations in the statistical conclusion validity, external validity, and construct validity categories are added as refinements to the basic evaluation research designs as circumstances dictate. Among the most powerful methods for controlling rival explanations in the construct validity category are (1) multiple operationalization, (2) placebo treatments, and (3) double blind experiments.[10] There are several techniques for increasing external validity: (1) random sampling; (2) use of heterogeneous groups of persons, settings and times; (3) generalization to modal instances; and (4) generalization to target instances.[11] The rival explanations in the statistical conclusion category are controlled through the creative and correct use of statistical techniques.

For the sake of brevity, a discussion will be presented here of only seven basic evaluation research designs. Most of the other designs are variations or elaborations of the designs which are discussed. The seven basic designs were selected because of their potential relevance for development specialists. The focus of the discussion is on the control of explanations in the internal validity category. Only the most simple versions of the basic evaluation research designs are presented.

One group posttest-only design. The basis of this design is a single posttreatment observation for the impact variable. It can be diagramed in the following manner:

$$X \quad O$$

where O is the observation or measure of the impact variable and X is the treatment (e.g., development activity). The problems with this frequently used preexperimental design are: (1) it does not allow for the detection of a pretest-posttest change or a treatment-nontreatment comparison; and (2) it does not control any of the plausible rival explanations in the internal validity category. It is the weakest of all designs for testing impact hypotheses.

One group pretest-posttest design. This design utilizes pretest data collected for the period before the treatment and posttest data collected for the period after the treatment:

$$O_1 \quad X \quad O_2$$

where O is the observation or measure of the impact variable and X is the treatment. This frequently used preexperimental design is stronger than the previous design because it makes possible the detection of a pretest-posttest change in the value of the impact variable. It is still very inadequate. The history, maturation, testing, and statistical regression explanations usually present serious problems when this design is used. There is a quasi-experimental separate sample pretest-posttest design which is somewhat similar and might be used in certain circumstances. Unfortunately, it is also quite limited in regard to possible causal inferences.

Posttest-only design with nonequivalent groups. This design utilizes a single posttreatment observation for the impact variable for both the treatment group and a nonrandomly selected control group:

$$\frac{X \quad O}{O}$$

where O is the observation or measure of the impact variable and X is the treatment. This design makes possible the comparison of a group of cases where a certain activity has been undertaken and a group of cases where a different activity or no activity has occurred. The selection and interactions with selection explanations make this preexperimental design weak. It is used frequently in social science research (many correlational studies are of this type), but it usually does not allow strong causal inferences.

Untreated control group design with pretest and posttest. This design utilizes pretest and posttest data for both a group which received the treatment and one which did not:

$$\frac{O_1 \quad X \quad O_2}{O_1 \quad\quad O_2}$$

where O is the observation or measure of the impact variable and X is the treatment. The treatment and control groups have not been equated through the use of randomization. This quasi-experimental design can be seen as a combination of the preexperimental posttest-only design with nonequivalent groups and the preexperimental one group pretest-posttest design. It is a stronger design than either of them. If the treatment has any impact, there should be a difference in the change observed for the groups. The statistical regression, interactions with selection, and local history explanations are difficult to control when this design is used. There are regression discontinuity, counterbalanced, and separate-sample pretest-posttest control group quasi-experimental designs which are somewhat similar and might be used in the development context.

Interrupted time-series design. The basis of the interrupted time-series design is the existence of periodic observations for the impact variable and the introduction of a treatment at some point:

$$O_1 \quad O_2 \quad O_3 \quad O_4 \quad X \quad O_5 \quad O_6 \quad O_7 \quad O_8$$

where O is the observation or measure of the impact variable (the number of data points may vary) and X is the treatment. This quasi-experimental design can be seen as the extension over time of the one group pretest-posttest design. It has the advantage of facilitating identification of an interruption in the data pattern and the comparison of trends before and after the intervention. The history explanation is especially difficult to control when this design is used. The cross-lagged panel design and the quasi-experimental equivalent time samples and equivalent material samples designs are somewhat similar and also might be useful in a particular circumstance.

Interrupted time-series design with a nonequivalent no-treatment control group time-series. The basis of this design is the existence of periodic observations for the impact variable for two groups and the introduction of a treatment at some point for one of the groups:

$$O_1 \quad O_2 \quad O_3 \quad O_4 \quad X \quad O_5 \quad O_6 \quad O_7 \quad O_8$$
$$\overline{O_1 \quad O_2 \quad O_3 \quad O_4 \qquad\quad O_5 \quad O_6 \quad O_7 \quad O_8}$$

where O is the observation or measure of the impact variable (the number of data points may vary) and X is the treatment. The treatment and control groups have not been equated through the use of randomization. This quasi-experimental design has the virtues of the interrupted time-series design and adds controls available through an untreated control group design with pretest and posttest. It facilitates the control of all rival explanations presenting challenges to the internal validity of a study.[12] The quasi-experimental institutional cycle and interrupted time-series with switching replications designs are somewhat similar and might be appropriate for use in some settings.

Pretest-posttest control group design. This is the classical experimental design. It employs pretest and posttest data for a group which received the treatment and one which did not:

$$O_1 \quad X \quad O_2$$

$$O_1 \qquad O_2$$

where O is the observation or measure of the impact variable and X is the treatment. If the treatment had any impact there should be a difference in the change observed for the groups. This design differs from the untreated control group design with pretest and posttest in that the groups have been equated through the use of randomization. Many of the rival explanations in the internal validity category are ruled out by proper use of the process of randomization. This design facilitates the control of all rival explanations presenting challenges to the internal validity of a study. It should be used whenever feasible. In some situations the Solomon four-group or the posttest-only control group designs, both of which are randomized experimental designs, might be used in the development context.

Different designs, of course, will be useful in different circumstances. Evaluation researchers are encouraged to be flexible in selecting relevant designs or in creating patched-up designs which are appropriate for use in specific circumstances.[13] The normal social science measurement, data collection, and data analysis procedures are available for use with these designs. A few comments are now in order regarding these matters because issues concerning their proper use are of the greatest importance.[14]

Measurement Concerns

The measurement process in an evaluation research study provides the crucial link between theoretical constructs and empirical data. Measurement is "the assignment of numerals to objects or events according to rules."[15] There are, of course, four scales of measurement (nominal, ordinal, interval, and ratio) and the level of measurement achieved reflects the precision of the measurement process. Each level of measurement carries with it a different set of properties, means different things, and has different rules for the assignment of numerals.

The reliability and validity problems are the most crucial ones in the measurement process. Reliability can mean the replicability of the instrument of measurement, the accuracy of the measurement process, or the amount of error contained in the instrument. The validity problem is a more difficult one and is concerned with whether "we are measuring what we think we are measuring."[16] Unless it is possible to depend upon the results of the measurement of constructs, it is not possible to have confidence in the examination of the relationship between constructs.

Systematic measurement procedures have been developed and are useful in attempts to minimize error. For example, scholars in the field of psychometric methods have been especially active in developing scaling and data reduction techniques which place the units of analysis along a dimension or dimensions in a manner which is consistent with the general concerns of measurement. Techniques such as factor analysis and discriminant function analysis have been used in the social sciences and are recommended for use when appropriate in evaluation research studies.[17]

It is generally accepted that relevant and meaningful measurement is advantageous in evaluation research studies. The major advantage is that the information from the empirical world is categorized or assigned a value which indicates its nature according to the specific criteria contained in the concepts of the researcher. How well particular constructs can be measured varies with circumstances. In the evaluation research approach the rival explanations in the construct validity category provide useful criteria for assessing the degree of adequacy of the measurement process employed in a particular study.

Data Collection Procedures

Regardless of which measurement rules or sources of data are utilized, the need is great for a rigorous and systematic data collection process. Various data collection techniques have been developed in the social sciences with the goal of providing relatively unbiased data. These techniques form part of the methodological arsenal for evaluation research studies.

Interviewing involves asking questions of individuals in an effort to obtain information regarding matters such as perceptions, attitudes, beliefs, and behavior. Interviewing techniques can be categorized according to the manner in which they are utilized: (1) structured or unstructured; (2) elite or mass; and (3) direct or mail.[18] Structured interviews involve the use of fixed questions asked in a particular sequence and with specific wording, while unstructured interviews are more open and flexible. When comparability of data from respondents is of primary importance, then structured interviewing would seem to be relevant. When specific substantive information, individual projection, or access to other data sources is the goal, unstructured interviewing may be more appropriate. Mass interviewing involves the collection of information from individuals selected from a large population and great emphasis is placed on the representativeness of the sample. It is rare that anything except a structured interview will be used in mass interviewing. Elite interviewing involves the questioning of individuals who hold special positions. Depending on the information being sought, the interview may be structured or unstructured. Interview information may be collected in person or through the use of a mail questionnaire. Quite obviously, the structured instrument, perhaps with some open-ended questions, is required in the use of mail questionnaires since the interviewer cannot interact with the respondent and probe interesting responses.

Another way of obtaining information is by watching individuals do and say things and by systematically recording this behavior. This is a particularly useful approach for examining behavior in public places or for gathering information on the performance of tasks. Observational methods yield information that is frequently independent of the willingness of the subjects to cooperate with a researcher. The observational techniques may be tightly structured or quite unstructured and the advantages and disadvantages of the formality of the instrument are approximately the same as in the case of interviewing.[19] Among the items which are observed frequently are participants, setting, and behavioral patterns. The presence of the observer may be known or unknown to the actors and he may be a participant or nonparticipant in the action. The specific type of observation and its use depends on the particular research problem. In recent years the use of unobtrusive measures of behavior has been emphasized.

Documentary materials are produced by organizations and individuals and they are available for evaluation research purposes. These materials include personal documents, newspapers, periodicals, statistical records, and both published and unpublished reports. (Social indicator systems are usually based on documentary materials.) There are several advantages in using documentary sources: (1) since the data are collected periodically, analysis over time is possible; (2) the cooperation of the actors is not required, as in the case of interviewing and sometimes observational techniques; and (3) since the interaction between the behavior and the researchers is nonexistent, the effect on the behavior by the researchers is minimized. The systematic retrieval of information from records or documents requires some type of fixed instrument if the data are to be comparable, and content analysis and coding techniques are used frequently for this purpose. Content analysis is a technique for the description of the content of communication.[20] In its simplest form, categories are established and the frequency of occurrence of categories is counted. One can content analyze materials in writing such as letters, diaries, newspaper articles, reports, speeches, and minutes of meetings. The major problems with the use of content analysis involve the establishment of the fixed instrument and the high cost of its application. Coding is "the technical procedure by which data are categorized and transformed into symbols."[21] Coding may be done after interviewing or observational data are collected or can be used in working with secondary sources. The problems involved in coding are generally similar to those of the content analysis technique and intercoder reliability is of the greatest importance.

The data collection procedures employed in an evaluation research study are important because the data become the empirical evidence used in the examination of the impact hypothesis. Assessing the data collection process requires a consideration of both the data sources and data collection techniques. Of course, the crucial question is: were the data sources and data collection techniques appropriate for the impact hypothesis being examined? In the evaluation research approach various rival explanations provide criteria for assessing the degree of adequacy of the data collection process employed in a particular study.

Data Analysis Techniques

The data analytic and statistical procedures employed in an evaluation research study will depend on the design used and the nature of the available data. The operations that can be performed on data depend on the measurement level and the manner in which the variables are related. Different routines have been developed for use with various measurement scales and combinations of variables. For example, analysis of variance and covariance techniques are appropriate for many randomized studies,[22] variations of the general regression model[23] or Box-Jenkins autoregressive integrated moving average (ARIMA) techniques [24] are employed for many quasi-experimental studies involving time-series data, and multiple regression[25] or causal modeling techniques[26] are useful for many correlational studies.

The role of data and statistical analysis in evaluation research is an important but limited one. Data analysis procedures are most frequently used for three purposes: (1) to describe individual variables; (2) to describe the relationship between variables; and (3) to estimate the probability of obtaining the results. These analyses provide ways of evaluating whether the available data support the impact hypotheses.

From a strict statistical standpoint there appear to be significant unresolved data analysis and statistical problems inherent in the use of certain evaluation research designs. A perspective will need to be developed for each study as to whether adequate techniques are available and whether in relation to other methodological difficulties the data analysis and statistical problems are critical. The really important question is: were the data and statistical analyses appropriate, on balance, for a specific empirical examination of the impact hypothesis? In the evaluation research approach the rival explanations in the statistical conclusion validity category provide useful criteria for assessing the degree of adequacy of the data analytic and statistical procedures.

Summary and Conclusions

Numerous measurement, data collection, and data analysis techniques and a variety of research designs combine to provide a flexible methodology for the rigorous empirical examination of impact hypotheses and the control of plausible rival hypotheses regarding the effectiveness of social action programs. Evaluation research implies the use of opportunism, innovation, cleverness, and creativity in handling research problems and doing the best feasible job in a particular circumstance.

There undoubtedly will be a division of labor as evaluation research is applied in the development context. This means that there will be varying degrees of interest in various aspects of the evaluation research enterprise by different individuals. Some readers may find the treatment of evaluation research methodology that is provided here to be adequate for their purposes, preferring to rely on others for methodological expertise. Others may want more information, and it is recommended that they examine the statements by Donald T. Campbell, Julian C. Stanley, and Thomas D. Cook, and that they select additional readings from among the publications by Campbell and his coauthors.[27] The individual who desires extensive elaboration on the methodology of evaluation research is encouraged to consult the citations provided in the notes or to begin a more comprehensive study by starting with the items selected for inclusion in the bibliography.

The real understanding of the worth of the evaluation research approach will come in the use of the methodology in the study of development activities. However, it can be anticipated that there will be significant applied research and research utilization problems. Before focusing explicitly on these potential problems, I would like to explore some of the nuances of the use of the methodology and demonstrate its relevance by presenting case studies of the use of the evaluation research methodology for the examination of development activities.

NOTES

1. Fred N. Kerlinger, *Foundations of Behavioral Research: Educational and Psychological Inquiry* (New York: Holt, Rinehart and Winston, 1966): 20.

2. The types of validity, rival explanations, and research designs discussed here were originally presented in Thomas D. Cook and Donald T. Campbell, "The design and conduct of quasi-experiments and true experiments in field settings," in M.D. Dunnette, ed., *Handbook of Industrial and Organizational Research* (Chicago: Rand McNally, 1976): 223-326; and Donald T. Campbell and Julian C. Stanley, *Experimental and Quasi-Experimental Designs for Research* (Chicago: Rand McNally, 1963). The terminology is that of those authors.

3. For elaboration on the types of validity and the rival explanations see Cook and Campbell, ibid.: 224-246.

4. Cook and Campbell, ibid.: 245.

5. Donald T. Campbell, "Reforms as experiments," *American Psychologist* 24 (1969): 411.

6. H. Laurence Ross, Donald T. Campbell, and Gene V. Glass, "Determining the social effects of a legal reform: the British 'Breathalyser' crackdown of 1967," *American Behavioral Scientist* 13 (1970): 495.

7. Cook and Campbell, "The design and conduct of quasi-experiments and true experiments in field settings": 229.

8. Cook and Campbell, ibid.: 245-298; and Campbell and Stanley, *Experimental and Quasi-Experimental Designs for Research.*

9. These design types differ primarily in regard to their control of explanations in the internal validity category. Experimental designs equate treatment and control groups by randomization, thereby isolating the effect of the treatment and helping to rule out numerous rival explanations in the internal validity category. The use of time-series data and nonequivalent control group data is frequent in the quasi-experimental designs. These designs are suggested for use when the more powerful experimental designs are not feasible. Preexperimental designs do not use randomization and make insufficient use of the quasi-experimental controls. They are designs of last resort.

10. Cook and Campbell, "The design and conduct of quasi-experiments and true experiments in field settings": 238-245.

11. Cook and Campbell, ibid.: 234-48.

12. Both this design and the interrupted time-series design are most powerful when the impact is abrupt and involves a pretest-posttest ($O_4 - O_5$) change because plausible rival explanations are more easily controlled for a short period.

13. For elaboration of the design ideas presented in this section see: Campbell and Stanley, *Experimental and Quasi-Experimental Designs for Research;* Campbell, "Reforms as experiments"; Donald T. Campbell and H. Laurence Ross, "The Connecticut crackdown on speeding: time series data in quasi-experimental analysis," *Law and Society Review* 3 (1968): 33-53; Ross, Campbell, and Glass, "Determining

the social effects"; Henry Riecken, Robert F. Boruch, Donald T. Campbell, Nathan Caplan, Thomas K. Glennan, Jr., John W. Pratt, Albert Rees, and Walter Williams, *Social Experimentation: A Method for Planning Social Intervention* (New York: Academic Press, 1974); Donald T. Campbell, "Assessing the impact of planned social change," in Gene M. Lyons, ed., *Social Research and Public Policies: The Dartmouth/OECD Conference* (Hanover, N.H.: University Press of New England, 1975); and Cook and Campbell, "The design and conduct of quasi-experiments and true experiments in field settings."

14. For elaboration on these matters, see Francis W. Hoole, "The behavioral science orientation to the study of international administration," in Robert S. Jordan, ed., *Multinational Cooperation: Economic, Social, and Scientific Development* (New York: Oxford University Press, 1972): 327-364.

15. S. Stevens as quoted in Kerlinger, *Foundations of Behavioral Research:* 411.

16. Kerlinger, ibid.: 444.

17. Cf., Rudolph J. Rummel, "Understanding factor analysis," *Journal of Conflict Resolution* 11 (1967): 444-480; William W. Cooley and Paul R. Lohnes, *Multivariate Data Analysis* (New York: John Wiley, 1971): 243-286; Jum C. Nunnally and William H. Wilson, "Method and Theory for Developing Measures in Evaluation Research," in Elmer L. Struening and Marcia Guttentag, eds., *Handbook of Evaluation Research,* Volume 1 (Beverly Hills, California: Sage Pub. 1975): 227-288; and Jum C. Nunnally and Robert L. Durham, "Validity, reliability, and special problems of measurement in evaluation research," in Struening and Guttentag, eds., *Handbook of Evaluation Research:* 289-352.

18. Cf., Charles H. Backstrom and Gerald D. Hursh, *Survey Research* (Evanston, Ill.: Northwestern University Press, 1963); Lewis A. Dexter, *Elite and Specialized Interviewing* (Evanston, Illinois: Northwestern University Press, 1970); and, Carol H. Weiss, "Interviewing in evaluation research," in Struening and Guttentag, eds., *Handbook of Evaluation Research:* 355-395.

19. Cf., Howard S. Becker, "Problems of inference and proof in participant observation," *American Sociological Review* 23 (1958): 652-660; and Claire Selltiz, Marie Jahoda, Morton Deutsch, and Stuart W. Cook, *Research Methods in Social Relations* (New York: Holt, Rinehart and Winston, 1961): 200-234.

20. Cf., Ole R. Holsti, *Content Analysis for the Social Sciences and Humanities* (Reading, Mass.: Addison-Wesley, 1969).

21. Selltiz et al., *Methods in Social Relations:* 401.

22. Cf., William L. Hays, *Statistics for Psychologists* (New York: Holt, Rinehart and Winston, 1963).

23. Cf., J. Johnston, *Econometric Methods* (Tokyo: McGraw-Hill Kogakusha, Ltd., 1972): 8-321.

24. Cf., G.E.P. Box and G.M. Jenkins, *Time Series Analysis: Forecasting and Control* (San Francisco: Holden-Day, 1970).

25. Cf., Jacob Cohen, "Multiple regression as a general data-analytic system," in Struening and Guttentag, eds., *Handbook of Evaluation Research:* 571-595.

26. Cf., Hubert M. Blalock, *Causal Models in the Social Sciences* (Chicago: Aldine, 1971); Donald S. Van Meter and Herbert S. Asher, "Causal perspectives on policy analysis," in Frank P. Scioli and Thomas J. Cook, eds., *Methodologies for Analyzing Public Policies* (Lexington, Mass.: Lexington Books, 1975): 61-72; and Thomas R. Dye and Neuman F. Pollack, "Path analytic models in policy research," in Scioli and Cook, eds., *Methodologies for Analyzing Public Policies:* 113-122.

27. Cf., Campbell and Stanley, *Experimental and Quasi-Experimental Designs*

for Research; Cook and Campbell, "The design and conduct of quasi-experiments and true experiments in field settings"; Donald T. Campbell, "Reforms as experiments"; Campbell and Ross, "The Connecticut crackdown on speeding"; Ross, Campbell, and Glass, "Determining the social effects"; Riecken et al., *Social Experimentation;* Campbell, "Assessing the impact of planned social change"; Donald T. Campbell and Robert F. Boruch, "Making the case for randomized assignments to treatments by considering the alternatives: six ways in which quasi-experimental evaluations in compensatory education tend to underestimate effects," in Carl A. Bennett and Arthur A. Lumsdaine, *Evaluation and Experiment: Some Critical Issues in Assessing Social Programs* (New York: Academic Press, 1975): 195-296; Donald T. Campbell and Albert Erlebacher, "How regression artifacts in quasi-experimental evaluations can mistakenly make compensatory education look harmful," in J. Hellmuth, ed., *Compensatory Education: A National Debate,* Volume 3, *Disadvantaged Child* (New York: Brunner/Mazel, 1970): 185-210; and Donald T. Campbell and Albert Erlebacher, "Reply to the Replies," in Hellmuth, ed., *Compensatory Education:* 221-225.

Chapter 2

USING TIME-SERIES DATA

Sometimes, by simply being innovative, it is possible to expand a data set for an impact variable over time, thereby strengthening greatly an evaluation research study. In general, the longer the time-series of data for the impact variable, the stronger the causal inferences that are possible. In fact, one of the most important means of controlling plausible rival hypotheses is through the use of both pre- and post-treatment time-series data, and several evaluation research designs are based upon such a strategy. These designs represent improvements over weaker designs simply because of the use of such data. We have in the advice, "expand your data base over time before and after the treatment" a classic case of a very simple idea being a very powerful one.

This idea is one of the most important ones found in evaluation research. In this chapter I shall demonstrate why this is so by showing how time-series data can be used to improve evaluation research studies in the development context. Information on the worldwide smallpox eradication program of the World Health Organization (WHO) is used to demonstrate how the control of rival explanations increases through the use of time-series data.

The WHO Smallpox Eradication Program

A smallpox attack begins with a fever and general aching. A rash then develops on various parts of the body. There is no cure for smallpox and approximately 30 percent of those who catch the disease die from it. Survivors are essentially immune from further attack. Fortunately smallpox is passed only from person to person and most individuals can transmit it only during a two week period. There is a vaccine, developed in 1796, which is quite successful in protecting persons from catching smallpox. Because of these factors, smallpox is the most susceptible to eradication of the infectious diseases. It is easily identified, and there is a feasible means of breaking the chain of transmission.

Smallpox was once endemic throughout the world. During the first half of the twentieth century both Europe and North America became essentially free from it. The 1950s saw the same result achieved in several African, Asian, and Latin American countries. The threat of reintroduction of smallpox into these countries and the relative ease with which it can be contained led the assembly of the World Health Organization in 1958 to call for the global eradication of the disease. Unfortunately, there was no increase in the resources available in the WHO regular budget for this task. Voluntary contributions were invited but the response was limited. There was little apparent impact as a result of the 1958 action by the WHO assembly.

In 1966 the member states of WHO decided to conduct an intensified worldwide smallpox eradication program with significantly increased financial resources to be made available through the regular budget of WHO.[1] It was felt that a coordinated global effort of increased technical assistance could eradicate the disease from the world in ten years. No insurmountable technical problems were foreseen, and the failure of countries to eliminate smallpox on their own was viewed as resulting principally from a lack of funds and organization failures in establishing surveillance and vaccination activities. The goal of the WHO intensified worldwide smallpox eradication program was a "zero incidence of small-pox."[2]

When the intensified program was begun in January of 1967, smallpox was endemic in thirty African, Asian, and Latin American countries. Fourteen additional countries had imported cases during 1967. Most projects in the endemic countries were begun during the first two years of the intensified effort. The last was started in 1971. Since January of 1967 WHO projects have been conducted in fifty different countries and the incidence of smallpox has declined steadily. Forty-four countries reported smallpox cases in 1967. Only two countries did so in 1976. It now appears that smallpox was virtually eliminated from the world during 1976, exactly ten years after the beginning of the intensified worldwide smallpox eradication program.[3]

The intensified WHO smallpox eradication program was built on several important technical and administrative innovations.[4] One important technical breakthrough involved the creation of a stable freeze-dried vaccine. Another resulted from the widespread use of jet injector guns and bifurcated needles. The most important technical innovation involved the use of containment rather than mass vaccination campaigns. Administrative innovations followed from several nontechnical lessons learned during the course of the program. These included recognition of (1) the need for modern management expertise in running the program; (2) the ecological unity between contiguous countries; and (3) the necessity of cooperation between countries. The Director-General of the World Health Organization, Halfdan Mahler, recently commented: "The eradication of smallpox will represent one of the historic milestones in medicine but, more than that, this first global eradication of a major disease provides an outstanding example of the constructive results nations can achieve when they work together toward the common cause of better health for all."[5]

It was estimated in 1975 that the countries with smallpox eradication programs had spent approximately 200 million dollars, and that international aid had amounted to another fifty million dollars. Of the latter amount roughly twenty-two million dollars came from the WHO regular budget, fourteen million dollars came from the government of the United States, eight million dollars came from the government of the USSR, and the remainder (six million dollars) was contributed by governments of other countries. Thus, through 1974 the most impressive program in the history of public health had cost approximately 250 million dollars. Surely the program was a bargain.[6]

Evaluation Research Considerations

The initial step in an evaluation research study is the determination of the impact hypotheses. It is the usual practice to begin by identifying which aspects of the program or activity are to be evaluated and by developing multiple indicators for program goals and possible side effects. This process will usually lead to the examination of a wide variety of impact hypotheses. However, I will keep things simple, and a single impact hypothesis will be evaluated for the purpose of the illustration in this chapter. The examination of multiple hypotheses would mean that several studies such as the one reported here would be conducted.

There are various aspects of the worldwide smallpox eradication program that deserve systematic evaluation. It would be interesting to compare systematically the relative effectiveness of mass and containment vaccination campaigns or jet injector guns and bifurcated needles. For this illustration the overall intensified program is evaluated. The independent variable is the smallpox eradication program of the World Health Organization. Among the most interesting indicators for assessing the impact of the smallpox program would be the number of deaths from smallpox in the world, number of smallpox cases in the world, and number of countries reporting smallpox cases. For this illustration a single indicator is used. This study utilizes as the dependent variable the number of countries in the world reporting smallpox cases. The impact hypothesis is: The intensified worldwide smallpox eradication program of the World Health Organization resulted in a reduction in the number of countries in the world reporting cases of smallpox.

The operational procedures are straightforward. The intensified WHO smallpox program began on January 1, 1967. The period prior to 1967 is considered to be the no-treatment era. The period after that is considered to be the treatment era. Annual data for the impact variable, the number of countries in the world reporting cases of smallpox, were obtained from the office of the chief of the WHO smallpox eradication unit.[7] There may be some error in these data. However, they appear to be generally reliable. They do have the virtue of being the best data available and were used by policy makers in the World Health Organization.

There are, of course, numerous interesting questions regarding the WHO smallpox eradication program which are not addressed here. Nevertheless, it does appear that the impact hypothesis being examined is an important one and that the operational procedures that are utilized are adequate for a fair empirical test of it. The discussion here provides examples of the application of different evaluation research designs to existing data. In an actual study only the most powerful possible design would be used and more data and additional impact hypotheses undoubtedly would be examined.

In any evaluation research study the research design should allow for a meaningful empirical examination of the impact hypothesis while ruling out as many rival explanations as possible. However, the choice of the design is limited by the nature of the data that can be utilized. Experimental designs cannot be employed here because randomization was not used in the choice of countries to receive the treatment. The use of quasi-experimental designs employing nonequivalent control group data is not feasible because the program was made worldwide when it was initiated. The evaluation research design utilizing time-series data is the most powerful feasible design, and it will be employed. However, the discussion will work its way up to the design employing time-series data by first considering weaker evaluation research designs. It should be noted that in an actual evaluation research study some of the design limitations discussed here might be overcome by planning the evaluation research study before the treatment is given, instead of retrospectively as in this instance.

One Group Posttest-Only Design

The basis of this design is a single posttest observation for the impact variable:

X   O

where O is the observation or measure of the impact variable and X is the treatment.

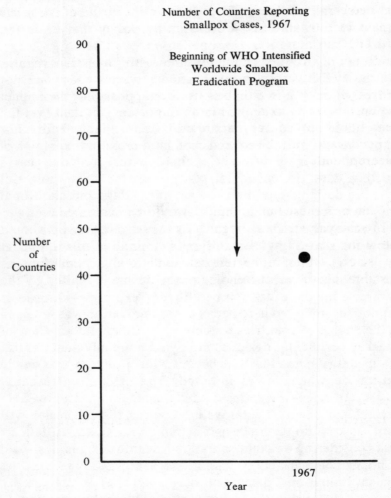

Figure 2.1: One Group Posttest-Only Design

When this design is used for the evaluation of the impact hypothesis, the X is the program initiated on January 1, 1967 and the O is the number of countries reporting smallpox cases during 1967. This information is presented in Figure 2.1.

One problem with this evaluation research design is that it does not allow the determination of whether the WHO smallpox eradication program had an impact on the number of countries reporting smallpox cases because it does not allow the detection of a pretest-posttest change. The specified impact hypothesis cannot be examined when this design is utilized. Furthermore, the one group posttest-only design would not control any of the plausible rival hypotheses in the internal validity category. It should be clear that any analysis utilizing this design would be a weak one. It is unfortunate that this design seems to be relied upon frequently in the development field.[8] Given the data which are available here, this design would not be considered in an actual evaluation research study.

One Group Pretest-Posttest Design

What happens when a single data point is added for the year before the program was begun? The answer is that we have a one group pretest-posttest design. The basis of this design is the use of pretest and posttest data to determine whether there was a change in value for the impact variable:

$$O_1 \quad X \quad O_2$$

where O is the observation or measure of the impact variable and X is the treatment.

When this design is used for the evaluation of the impact hypothesis, the X is the program initiated on January 1, 1967, O_1 is the number of countries reporting smallpox cases during 1966, and O_2 is the number of countries reporting smallpox cases during 1967. This information is presented in Figure 2.2. As can be seen, there was no change in the number of countries reporting smallpox cases during the first year of the intensified program. Forty-four countries reported cases during both 1966 and 1967. This particular empirical test of the impact hypothesis does not reveal the anticipated impact.

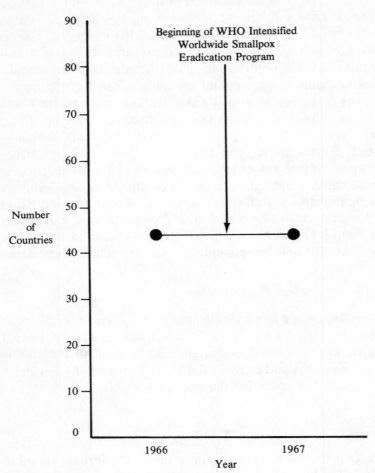

Figure 2.2: One Group Pretest-Posttest Design

This design is stronger than the one group posttest-only design because it makes possible the detection of a pretest-posttest change in the impact variable. It is ,however, still very inadequate and should not be mistaken for a powerful evaluation research design. Even if the design would have indicated that the smallpox eradication program impact hypothesis had empirical support, in this circumstance it would not have ruled out the history, maturation, testing and statistical regression explanations in the internal validity category.

Those rival hypotheses would have presented plausible explanations for the observed impact.[9] It should be clear why Thomas D. Cook and Donald T. Campbell call this design "uninterpretable."[10]

A further problem with this use of the design lies in the fact that it requires that a program or activity be fully introduced at one time and that the effect be of an immediate nature. The WHO smallpox eradication program, like so many other complex social action programs in the development field, took an extended period of time to become fully operational and for the impact to be felt. Most projects in the endemic countries were begun during the first two years of the intensified effort and the last was not started until 1971. Furthermore, in most countries it took more than a year to eradicate smallpox. This use of the one group pretest-posttest design did not allow adequately for the capturing of the impact of the program because it measured only the impact between 1966 and 1967.

Interrupted Time-Series Design

If the one group pretest-posttest design is extended through the addition of data points before and after the beginning of the program, then an interrupted time-series design is obtained:

$$O_1 \quad O_2 \quad O_3 \quad O_4 \quad X \quad O_5 \quad O_6 \quad O_7 \quad O_8$$

where O is the observation or measure of the impact variable (the number of data points may vary) and X is the treatment. This quasi-experimental design is most powerful when the impact is of an abrupt nature and can be noted as a pretest-posttest ($O_4 - O_5$) change because plausible rival explanations are more easily controlled for a short period. However, the design is well worth undertaking when the expected change is of a longer term nature as in the case of the WHO smallpox eradication program.

When the interrupted time-series design is used for the evaluation of the impact hypothesis, the X is the program initiated on January 1, 1967 and the O's are the number of countries reporting smallpox cases for various years. Annual

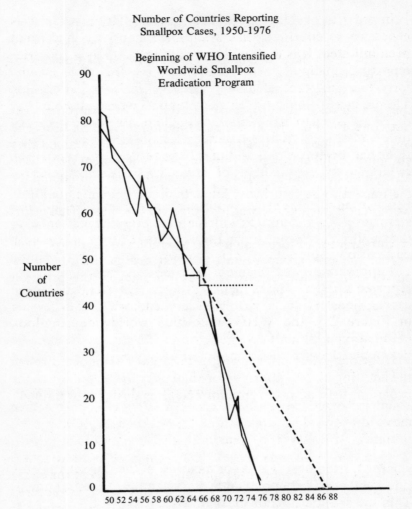

Number of Countries Reporting
Smallpox Cases, 1950-1976

Figure 2.3: Interrupted Time-Series Design

data on the number of smallpox cases for 1950-1976 are presented in Figure 2.3. The number of countries reporting smallpox cases fluctuated downward prior to 1967. The number of countries decreased from a high of eighty-two in 1950 to a low of forty-four in 1966. After the intensified program was begun, the number of countries reporting cases decreased from forty-four in 1967 to two in 1976.

In order to evaluate the impact of the WHO program it is necessary to consider what would have happened had it not been initiated. It is highly likely that the number of countries reporting smallpox cases would have leveled off at around forty-four and fluctuated near that level for a period of time. This scenario would reflect the situation where all countries that were going to bring smallpox under control for a period of time had done so. This scenario reflects the viewpoint that a floor had been reached and that little further progress in the reduction of the number of countries reporting cases of smallpox could be anticipated. This scenario seems realistic because many of the states reporting cases of smallpox in 1966 were developing countries with far more pressing matters than the smallpox problem, and many were doing little serious work on their own to eradicate smallpox. The dotted line in figure 2.3 approximates the number of countries that would have reported smallpox cases if this scenario had been true. If the assumptions of this scenario are accepted, then, as can be seen in Figure 2.3, the WHO intensified worldwide smallpox eradication program had an enormous impact, and it must be concluded that there is strong empirical support for the impact hypothesis.

A less likely scenario is that the trend in the number of countries reporting smallpox cases would have continued to move downward at approximately the same rate after the initiation of the WHO intensified smallpox eradication program as before it was begun. Thus, under this assumption smallpox would have been eliminated after 1966 at the same rate as before, presumably as public health infrastructures were developed in countries in the course of normal events. It is, of course, impossible to say definitely what would have happened had the WHO intensified program not been undertaken. It does seem reasonable to use the extension of the past trend as a benchmark against which to evaluate the impact of the WHO smallpox eradication program, at least as long as it is biased against the detection of the full impact of the WHO program.

The years were regressed on the number of countries to determine the linear trends. The dummy variable strategy of Gujarti[11] was used:

$$Y_t = a + b_1 X_t + b_2 D_t + b_3 (X_t \cdot D_t) + e_t \quad (2.1)$$

where Y_t equals the number of countries reporting smallpox cases, X_t equals the years, D_t is a dummy variable with O used for the 1950-1966 time period and 1 for the 1967-1976 era, a is the intercept, the b's are fixed coefficients, and e is an error term that takes into account factors not otherwise included in the equation. A number of assumptions concerning the form of the model (linear), disturbances (zero mean, homoskedastic variance, nonautoregressive), and independent variables (stationary and independent of the disturbance term) must be satisfied for the parameters to be estimated using the general linear regression model and for the resulting estimates to be optimal (unbiased, efficient, and consistent).[12] All required assumptions, with the exception of the one concerning stationarity, are reasonable in this case.[13] Because of the importance of the assumption of nonautocorrelated error terms the Durbin-Watson d statistic[14] and the Theil-Nagar[15] .01 level for it were used to examine the first order independence of the disturbances. While the statistical techniques used do not offer optimal solutions to all problems, on balance they appear to be adequate for their purpose.[16]

The ordinary least squares technique provided satisfactory estimates (Durbin-Watson d=1.62) for equation (2.1).[17] The relevant information has been plotted in Figure 2.3. The trend for the 1950-1966 era indicates that the number of countries reporting smallpox cases decreased at the average rate of 2.1 per year. An extrapolation of the trend for the 1950-1966 era (see Figure 2.3) indicates that smallpox would have been eradicated in twenty-one years, in 1987, had that trend continued. The trend for 1967-1976, the period after the start of the WHO program, indicates that the number of countries reporting cases decreased at an average of 4.6 per year. The average decrease in countries reporting cases is greater after the initiation of the WHO intensified program, and the difference of 2.5 countries per year would be considered to be substantively significant by most observers, as would the savings of approximately a decade in the virtual eradication of smallpox from the world. Again there is strong empirical support for the impact hypothesis.

Is the change statistically significant? In order to answer that question the hypothesis that the coefficients describing the 1950-1966 era belong to the same regression as the coefficients describing the 1967-1976 era was examined through use of Chow's F test.[18] The value for the F ratio was 19.25, which is significant well beyond the .0001 level. Analysis of the tests for the intercept change and the slope change indicates that both of those changes were significant beyond the .0001 level.[19] The preintervention and postintervention trends are significantly different from a statistical standpoint.

Can the results that were observed for the WHO intensified smallpox eradication program be accounted for by other explanations? In order to answer this question we will turn to a consideration of the plausible rival hypotheses. The rival explanations in the external and construct validity categories will not be examined because there is no concern here with generalizing the observed results across times, settings, and persons or across treatments and measures. Some explanations in the internal validity category are not plausible because they concern differences in treatment and control groups. There is no control group utilized here. The remaining explanations in the internal validity category and those in the statistical conclusion group are examined for plausibility of explanation of the reduction in the number of countries reporting smallpox cases.

History. There was no other worldwide smallpox program which occurred during the 1967-1976 era and which might have produced the observed change in the trend in the number of countries reporting smallpox cases. Nevertheless, it would have been possible to have more faith in ruling out the history explanation if a control group design had been feasible because specific events occurring at the same time as the program could be expected to have affected both treatment and control group cases, and thus to have been controlled. If the program had been introduced abruptly and the impact immediate, then only other events during 1967, rather than the entire 1967-1976 era, could have had an effect. More faith in the ruling out of this explanation would have been possible in that circumstance.

Maturation. There may have been a maturation process operating in the public health field. As the delivery of medical care became more effective and as basic health infrastructures in countries became better established, the incidence of smallpox might have decreased naturally. However, it would appear to be unlikely that the maturation process would cause the observed change in the impact variable.

Testing. In the smallpox case the concern is with the effect of publicity regarding a social indicator on later values of that indicator. It seems defensible to assign a very low plausibility to the challenge presented by this explanation because of the nature of the indicator and the unlikely possibility that a testing effect would suddenly develop at the same time as the program.

Instrumentation. There was a change in the calibration of the measuring instrument because a major part of the WHO program involved setting up better surveillance systems. However, the instrumentation change would tend to work against the observed success of the program. After the WHO intensified program was initiated, it was less likely that cases of smallpox would go unreported. The increase in the number of countries during the 1950-1976 period also presents a potential instrumentation problem, but again the bias is against the observed success of the program. The decrease in the number of countries reporting smallpox cases is even more impressive because of changes in instrumentation.

Statistical regression. This explanation is concerned with a possible statistical artifact: "If the group was selected because it was extreme on some measure, statistical reasoning indicates that it will appear less extreme on subsequent tests, even though the intervening treatment may be completely ineffectual."[20] Had the WHO intensified program been initiated as a reaction to a crisis rather than to a chronic situation the prospect of the observed impact being an artifact would have been greater. This explanation seems unlikely because the trend in the number of countries reporting smallpox cases started down long before the intervention.

Ambiguity about the direction of causal inference. In this analysis it is possible to tell which variable is actually the cause and which variable is the effect because of the time-series design. This explanation is not possible here.

Statistical power. The observed results appear to be so clear that it is doubtful that a change in the sample size or level of significance would have produced a different conclusion. There is no opportunity for checking on this rival explanation by increasing the sample size because all of the available data were used. Had the sample been larger, it might have been possible to adapt for use in this study more sensitive statistical techniques such as the Box-Jenkins ARIMA methods.[21] Furthermore, it is hard to see how the hypothesis is one-sided. This rival explanation seems unlikely in this situation, although it is not ruled out.

Fishing and the error rate problem. This rival explanation seems unlikely because no searching was done for statistically significant cutting points. It is difficult to see how chance might have produced the observed statistical conclusion regarding impact.

The reliability of measures. There is a high degree of reliability in the impact measure utilized and it is difficult to see how lack of reliability could have produced the observed statistical conclusion. This explanation would have been quite plausible had an indicator such as number of cases of smallpox or number of deaths from smallpox been used because the reliability of those measures is low.

The reliability of treatment implementation. The lack of standardization of the implementation of the smallpox eradication program would tend to work against the observed statistical conclusion. This would appear to be a plausible explanation had a different unit of analysis been used or had no impact been observed.

Random irrelevancies in the experimental setting. In this analysis features of the experimental setting other than the treatment would tend to work against the production of the statistical conclusion regarding impact. This would appear to be a plausible explanation had no impact been observed.

Random heterogeneity of respondents. In this situation any heterogeneity of respondents with respect to variables that affect the impact variable would tend to work against the observed statistical conclusion. This rival explanation would appear to be plausible had no impact been observed.

After consideration of the relevant explanations there appears to be no highly plausible rival explanation for the observed results. Thus the impact hypothesis has received empirical support and has not been falsified convincingly. It is reasonable to conclude that the smallpox eradication program had a significant impact by reducing the number of countries in the world reporting smallpox cases. I am left with little doubt regarding the effectiveness of the program. It should be noted, however, that had I relied on the analysis of the one group pretest-posttest design that was reported earlier in the chapter, I would have concluded incorrectly that the WHO program had no impact.

Summary and Conclusions

The WHO smallpox program case study conveys how and why time-series data can be of assistance in controlling rival explanations in impact studies of development activities. Hopefully, the reader has learned how to move from the evaluation research design employing a single impact variable data point to one employing time-series data with several data points before and after the intervention, and that this change improves the strength of evaluation research studies because a more adequate test is possible of the impact hypothesis and because an additional number of plausible rival hypotheses can be controlled. Most evaluation research studies of development activities will be more complex than the one presented here and the impact will be less clear. The evaluation research approach will be of greater assistance in helping to sort out cause and effect in those cases.

Unfortunately, time-series designs are not without problems. There will be the usual potential applied research problems concerning the formulation of meaningful impact hypotheses, measurement concerns, and organizational resistances and special problems may arise concerning data availability and data analysis. Furthermore there are potential research utilization problems concerning factors such as the timing and relevance of studies employing time-series data. However, before examining these problems in detail let us consider other ways in which evaluation research studies can be strengthened. Only after that will we be in a position to discuss meaningfully the relative strengths, weaknesses, and implications of designs employing time-series data.

NOTES

1. For background on the WHO smallpox eradication program ,see *WHO Expert Committee on Smallpox*, 1st Report, World Health Organization Technical Report Series No. 283 (Geneva: World Health Organization, 1964); *Smallpox Eradication*, Report of a WHO Scientific Group, World Health Organization Technical Report Series No. 393 (Geneva: World Health Organization, 1968); *WHO Expert Committee on Smallpox Eradication,* 2nd Report, World Health Organization Technical Report No. 493 (Geneva: World Health Organization, 1972); special issue entitled "Smallpox: point of no return," *World Health* (February-March 1975); "Smallpox eradication," in *The Second Ten Years of the World Health Organization,* 1958-67 (Geneva: World Health Organization, 1968): 105-111; "Smallpox eradication programme," Annex 15, *Nineteenth World Health Assembly,* Part I, World Health Organization Official Records No. 151 (Geneva: World Health Organization, 1966): 106-121; "Smallpox," *Handbook of Resolutions and Decisions of the World Health Assembly and Executive Board,* Volume I, 1948-1972 (Geneva: World Health Organization, 1973): 89-97.

2. *WHO Expert Committee on Smallpox Eradication*, 2nd Report: 9.

3. WHO will declare the disease eradicated only after a two year period during which no cases are located. Smallpox cases during 1976 were reported only by Ethiopia and Somalia. Unfortunately the war in those countries has hindered the final push to eradicate smallpox in the world.

4. Cf., David J. Sencer, "Lessons for the future," *World Health* (February-March 1975): 18-21.

5. Halfdan Mahler, "Smallpox: point of no return," *World Health* (February-March 1975): 3.

6. All cost estimates were taken from F. J. Tomiche, "Fruits of victory,"*World Health* (February-March 1975): 26-28. The following information also was reported by Tomiche and indicates what a bargain the WHO program was for the United States. It has been estimated that 151 million dollars were spent in 1968 in protecting individuals from smallpox in the United States, even though there had not been a smallpox case in the U.S. for several years. In 1971 the WHO smallpox eradication program succeeded in eliminating smallpox from the Western hemisphere and compulsory smallpox vaccination was abolished in the United States. Most of the money being spent on the disease was saved. Because of the WHO smallpox eradication program the savings in the United States between 1971 and 1975 amounted to more than all of the contributions made by the United States government to the World Health Organization during the first quarter century of its existence.

7. I have used all of the years for which comparable data were available. I am especially grateful to Jacques Copland for his assistance in locating the data.

8. For an overview of family planning studies in the development field which have employed this design, see Elizabeth T. Hilton and Arthur A. Lumsdaine, "Field trial designs in gauging the impact of fertility planning programs," in Carl A. Bennett and

Arthur A. Lumsdaine, eds., *Evaluation and Experiment: Some Critical Issues in Assessing Social Programs* (New York: Academic Press, 1975): 359-362.

9. The testing hypothesis appears to be unlikely in this circumstance because of the nature of the indicator. The point here is that the one group pretest-posttest design does not automatically rule out this hypothesis and I do not have sufficient additional information to do so.

10. Thomas D. Cook and Donald T. Campbell, "The design and conduct of quasi-experiments and true experiments in field settings," in M.D. Dunnette, ed., *Handbook of Industrial and Organizational Research* (Chicago: Rand McNally, 1976): 246.

11. Damodar Gujarti, "Use of dummy variables in testing equality between sets of coefficients in two linear regressions: a note," *The American Statistician* 24,4 (1970): 50-52; and, Damodar Gujarti, "Use of dummy variables in testing for equality between sets of coefficients in linear regressions: a generalization," *The American Statistician* 24,5 (1970): 18-22.

12. For a general treatment of regression analysis see J. Johnston, *Econometric Methods* (Tokyo: McGraw-Hill Kogakusha, 1972).

13. Unfortunately the effect of the violation of the stationarity assumption is not well understood, although it is known that stationarity is necessary to establish certain desirable asymptotic properties of the regression estimates. J. Kmenta has shown however that the assumption is not necessary for consistency. See J. Kmenta, *Elements of Econometrics* (New York: Macmillan, 1971): 298.

14. J. Durbin and G.S. Watson, "Testing for serial correlation in least squares regression," Part I *Biometrika* 37 (1950): 409-428; and J. Durbin and G.S. Watson, "Testing for serial correlation in least squares regression," Part II, *Biometrika* 38 (1951): 159-178.

15. H. Theil and A.G. Nagar, "Testing the independence of regression disturbances," *Journal of the American Statistical Association* 56 (1961): 793-806.

16. I considered using Box-Jenkins techniques to analyze the data. However, I have only twenty-seven cases and it is recommended that fifty cases be available for use of these techniques (Cook and Campbell, "The design and conduct of quasi-experiments and true experiments in field settings": 275). I do feel comfortable working with linear trends in this case. Furthermore, I conducted checks on the error terms for a first order autoregressive scheme and a fifth order autoregressive scheme and I could detect no significant problem of autocorrelated error terms in either case (see note 17 for the details).

In the analysis reported in this chapter the estimates of regression coefficients (which are used to provide estimates of the trends) should be consistent even when the error terms are autocorrelated. Therefore, it would seem appropriate even in the face of autocorrelated error terms to use the estimates of the regression coefficients to determine the before and after intervention average annual changes in the number of countries reporting smallpox cases. If the error terms were autocorrelated, then the estimates for the regression coefficients would be inefficient and the use of tests of significance would not be appropriate. For elaboration on the effect of autocorrelated error terms, see Douglas A. Hibbs, Jr., "Problems of statistical estimation and causal inference in time-series regression models," in H.L. Costner, ed., *Sociological Methodology 1973-1974* (San Francisco: Jossey-Bass, 1974): 256-259, 265-266.

The data are reported in note 17, and I encourage others to consider analyzing them using Box-Jenkins techniques to determine how serious violation of the fifty case assumption would be in this circumstance and whether these techniques would produce different results. I hope to find the time in the future to return to this topic for a more detailed study. I do feel that the Box-Jenkins techniques are superior in many circumstances to the techniques employed here and that they should be used in evaluation research studies when it is appropriate.

For information on autoregressive integrated moving average models, see G.E.P. Box and G. M. Jenkins, *Time Series Analysis: Forecasting and Control* (San Francisco: Holden-Day, 1970); Thomas H. Naylor, Terry G. Seaks, and D. W. Wichern, "Box-Jenkins methods: an alternative to econometric models," *International Statistics Review* 40 (1972): 123-137; G.E.P. Box and G. C. Tiao, "A change in level of nonstationary time series," *Biometrika* 52 (1965): 181-192; Gene V. Glass, George C. Tiao, and Thomas O. Maguire, "The 1900 revision of German divorce laws: analysis of data as a time-series quasi-experiment," *Law and Society Review 6* (1971): 532-562; Charles R. Nelson, *Applied Time Series Analysis for Managerial Forecasting* (San Francisco: Holden-Day, 1973); Douglas A. Hibbs, Jr., "On analyzing the effects of policy interventions: Box-Jenkins and Box-Tiao vs. structural equation models," in D. Heise, ed., *Sociological Methodology 1977* (San Francisco: Jossey-Bass, 1977): 137-179; G.E.P. Box and G. C. Tiao, "Intervention analysis with applications to economic and environmental problems," *Journal of the American Statistical Association* 70 (1975): 70-79; Gene V. Glass, "Estimating the effects of intervention into a non-stationary time-series," *American Educational Research Journal* 9 (1972):463-477; Peter Lemieux, "Box-Jenkins models, quasi-experimental designs, and forecasting in international relations," paper prepared for delivery at the Annual Meetings of the International Studies Association, Royal York Hotel, Toronto, Canada, February 25-29, 1976; and Gene V. Glass, V. L. Wilson, and J. M. Gottman, *Design and Analysis of Time-Series Experiments* (Boulder, Colorado: Colorado Associated Press, 1975).

17. The statistical analysis reported in this chapter was done on the CDC 6600 computer at Indiana University. A revised version of the BMDO2R Program was prepared for this analysis by David H. Handley. I am most grateful to him.

The annual data on the number of countries in the world reporting cases of smallpox for 1950-1976 are as follows: 82, 81, 72, 71, 69, 63, 59, 68, 61, 61, 54, 56, 61, 54, 46, 46, 44, 44, 39, 31, 24, 16, 19, 11, 9, 4, and 2.

The following ordinary least squares estimates were obtained for equation (2.1):

$$a = 4189 \; (11.85)^{**} \qquad\qquad R^2 = .98$$
$$b_1 = -2.1 \; (11.67)^{**} \qquad\quad F = 365.20^{**}$$
$$b_2 = 5019 \; (5.79)^{**} \qquad\quad \text{D-W } d = 1.62^*$$
$$b_3 = -2.5 \; (-5.80)^{**}$$

where the t tests for the regression coefficients are in parentheses and * indicates no significance at the .01 level and ** indicates significance at the .0001 level.

In order to obtain an estimate of whether there is higher order autocorrelation of error terms, I examined the following equation:

$$e_t = a + b_1 e_{t-1} + b_2 e_{t-2} + b_3 e_{t-3} + b_4 e_{t-4} + b_5 e_{t-5} + u_t \qquad (2.2)$$

where the e's are the residuals generated by the ordinary least squares estimates of equation (2.1) and the u is an error term. The following ordinary least squares estimates were obtained for equation (2.2):

$$a = -0.32 \; (-0.37)^* \qquad\qquad b_5 = -0.07 \; (-0.31)^*$$
$$b_1 = 0.11 \; (0.45)^* \qquad\qquad R^2 = .10 \quad R = .31$$
$$b_2 = -0.18 \; (-0.71)^* \qquad\quad F = 0.34^*$$
$$b_3 = -0.21 \; (-0.85)^* \qquad\quad \text{D-W } d = 1.89^*$$
$$b_4 = 0.01 \; (0.06)^*$$

where the t tests for the regression coefficients are in parentheses and * indicates no significance at the .01 level. The relevant bivariate relationships among the lagged error terms were the following: $r_{t \cdot t-1} = .13$; $r_{t \cdot t-2} = -.17$; $r_{t \cdot t-3} = -.24$; $r_{t \cdot t-4} = -.01$; and, $r_{t \cdot t-5} = .01$.

There appears to be no significant problem with higher order autocorrelation of error terms.

18. G. C. Chow, "Tests of equality between sets of coefficients in two linear regressions," *Econometrica* 28 (1960): 591-605. The use of Chow's test in this circumstance involves regressing the years on the number of countries and comparing the results with those obtained where equation (2.1) is used.

The following ordinary least squares estimates were obtained for the regression of the years on the number of countries reporting cases of smallpox:

$$a = 5790 \ (20.36)** \qquad\qquad R^2 = .94$$
$$b = -2.9 \ (-20.20)** \qquad\quad F = 408.11**$$
$$\text{D-W } d = .61*$$

where t tests for the regression coefficients are in parentheses and * indicates significance at the .01 level and ** indicates significance at the .0001 level. Because of positively autocorrelated error terms the R^2, F and t values are inflated and should not be relied upon.

19. An analysis of the autocorrelation of error terms suggests also that the WHO program intervention had an impact. When the years are regressed on the number of countries reporting smallpox cases the Durbin-Watson d of .61 indicates first order autocorrelation of error terms at the .01 level and thus an incorrect specification of the model. When the intervention model represented by equation (2.1) is analyzed the Durbin-Watson d of 1.62 does not indicate first order autocorrelation of error terms at the .01 level and an incorrect specification of the model.

The fact that the significant autocorrelation of error terms is positive in the first case suggests that the unexplained sum of squares is underestimated in that circumstance and hence that the value of Chow's F is underestimated. In this study the F value is so significant that it does not really matter. I did not use generalized least squares (GLS) estimation procedures because of the difficulties in comparing GLS variance estimates with other GLS variance estimates or with those obtained using ordinary least squares techniques. My assessment of the impact of the WHO program is not tied exclusively to the use of Chow's F test and an unbiased estimate of it.

20. H. Laurence Ross, Donald T. Campbell, and Gene V. Glass, "Determining the social effects of a legal reform: the British 'Breathalyser' crackdown of 1967," *American Behavioral Scientist* 13 (1970): 495.

21. See note 16 for a discussion of this matter.

Chapter 3

USING NONEQUIVALENT CONTROL GROUP DATA

Another of the simple but clever ideas found in the evaluation research literature involves comparing impact variable changes for the treatment group (or groups) and a control group which did not receive the treatment. If the treatment had an effect, there should be a difference in those changes. When randomization is used to assign cases to treatment and control groups then the groups are considered to be equivalent and we have an experiment. When randomization is not used for the assignment of cases then the groups are considered to be nonequivalent. The use of randomization is preferable because it is the best method known for equating groups, thus convincingly controlling certain plausible rival explanations. However, it is frequently not possible to utilize randomization when creating treatment and control groups. Hence data from nonequivalent control groups are used. In fact, several evaluation research designs are based on such a strategy. These designs represent improvements over weaker designs because the use of nonequivalent control group data does provide some control of plausible rival hypotheses. When nonequivalent control group data and time-series data are used meaningfully in the same design then we have the strongest possible quasi-experimental design.

In this chapter I shall demonstrate how and why non-equivalent control group data can and should be used to improve evaluation research studies of development activities. Information on rice programs in Indonesia, Thailand, and Burma is used to demonstrate how the control of rival explanations increases through the addition of nonequivalent control group data.

The Indonesian Rice Program

The Indonesian government's interest in agricultural development dates back to the independence from Dutch colonial rule in 1949.[1] During the years following independence the government program emphasized transferring knowledge on agricultural techniques to farmers through agricultural and paddy centers. Because rice is by far the most important agricultural crop, special attention was devoted to it. In 1963 numerous village demonstration projects in methods of encouraging peasants to adopt more advanced techniques of rice cultivation were carried out. This soon led to a new national program, which reached its heights during the 1964-1967 period. The basis for the program was governmental dictation of the kind and amount of fertilizer and herbicides and their distribution in the form of a packet. Unfortunately, as the program developed, the governmental bureaucracy became rigid in the determination and implementation of agricultural directives and the peasants developed resistance to the program. Little increase in rice production per hectare was achieved.

In 1968 the Suharto government, which had officially taken office in 1967, began implementing a different strategy for the rice program. This strategy was based on use of the new high-yielding varieties of rice.[2] The primary goals were to raise rice production and improve peasant living standards. The program strategy during the period from 1968-1970, which has been labeled the era of the "miracle of the multinational corporation,"[3] was based upon reliance on external sources of expertise to compensate for the shortcoming of local institutions. During this period the primary responsibility for agricultural inputs was given to European-based multinational corporations with special emphasis being placed on aerial spraying. The peasants had little choice regarding use of these new services and were forced to accept responsibility for paying for them. While rice production was increasing, it soon became clear that the government was paying an enormous economic (because of the high expenses) and political (because of peasant resistance) cost for the program.

In the summer of 1970 the government changed its strategy. The use of green revolution technology was still the basis for the program but prominent use of outside companies stopped. The 1970 change, which has been labeled the "managerial revolution,"[4] allowed the peasant to determine and to control within certain limits the agricultural inputs to be used. Thus there was a partial move to the use of the market mechanism. As Gary E. Hansen noted: "The entire [managerial revolution] approach is implicitly predicated on the fact that, given the presence of certain economic incentives, the peasant will voluntarily take the initiative to increase his yields."[5] The Suharto government still seemed determined to bring the green revolution to Indonesia but was employing a different strategy in promoting it.

The basis for the green revolution can be found in the new high-yielding grain varieties.[6] They are semidwarf in nature and most were developed at the International Maize and Wheat Improvement Center (CIMMYT) in Mexico and International Rice Research Institute (IRRI) in the Philippines. The first widely successful IRRI rice variety, IR-8, was released to farmers in 1966. Rice varieties with greater resistance to insects and diseases, and with more desirable consumer qualities, have been developed and released since 1966. The most important biological feature of high-yielding rice is responsiveness to fertilizer. Other important characteristics include a short growing season, which makes multiple cropping possible, and the need for a constant water supply, which means the new varieties are most successful when controlled irrigation conditions are used. Under ideal circumstances the high-yielding rice varieties can produce about twice as much as local varieties.

Unfortunately, this potential is not always realized on a widespread basis by farmers. Scientists have created the means by which the yield of rice can be increased under controlled experimental conditions yet the challenge is in transferring this technology to the farmers and bringing about a significant nationwide increase in crop production. Numerous factors appear to be vital in determining the success or failure of a green revolution program: availability of high-yielding seeds, proper irrigation, fertilizer, ample credit, extension services, an adequate pricing and marketing system, and political stability. Even if these items are present, there are still potential second generation problems such as price shock, income distribution, and regional disparities which can undermine a program. The magnitude and complexity of support required to bring about a green revolution mean that in developing countries a strong commitment from the government in the form of a long term program accompanied by technical assistance from outside the country holds the most promise for bringing about the desired end. Governments are frequently prepared to make this commitment because of a number of potential benefits to be derived from a successful green revolution program: increased crop production, reduction of hunger, improvement in the balance of trade, increased national income, and increased employment.[7] The Suharto government appears to have been interested in these potential benefits when it adopted the green revolution technology for the Indonesian rice program in 1968.

Green revolution activities are the type of development activities that are most in need of systematic evaluation. They are complex and the impacts are not obvious. There are numerous goals and the understanding of which ones are achieved is difficult without a systematic evaluation. The green revolution activities are conducted on a large scale and the stakes are high. The expense of evaluation is a minor part of the overall program cost yet evaluation results could be of major significance. It is known how to increase agricultural production under controlled experimental conditions, but it is not known exactly how to increase the agricultural production of an entire country. There are, in short, important unanswered questions.

Evaluation Research Considerations

For the purpose of this illustration it was decided to focus on an impact hypothesis which is more generalizable and more conceptually oriented than the smallpox program impact hypothesis examined in Chapter 2. Thus concerns will arise here regarding the operationalizations as measures of concepts and the legitimacy of generalizing the findings to other circumstances. Hence construct validity and external validity matters are of concern, as are the types of internal validity and statistical conclusion validity matters discussed in the last chapter. The impact hypothesis to be examined is: national green revolution programs result in national increases in agricultural production. A national green revolution program is considered to be a national governmental agricultural program that utilizes the technology of the green revolution. National agricultural production is considered to be the production of agricultural goods within the country.

There are, of course, numerous aspects of national green revolution programs which deserve systematic evaluation. It would be meaningful to evaluate programs in their entirety, compare the effectiveness of different farmer cooperative strategies, study different ways for governments to prescribe and deliver seeds and fertilizers, examine different uses of outside expertise, and focus on the various contributions by outside technical assistance agencies. I decided to examine here the impact of the overall green revolution rice program and to focus on the Indonesian national program in its entirety. Among the more meaningful indicators for evaluating the impact of green revolution activities would be overall agricultural production, individual crop production, agricultural imports, caloric intake, changes in income equality, and small farmer income. However, only a single impact indicator will be used here and it was decided to focus on annual data on rice yield in kilograms per hectare.[8] There are numerous interesting questions regarding green revolution activities that are not addressed. They could serve as the basis for additional studies utilizing the evaluation research methodology to examine different impact hypotheses.

Because the primary purpose here is the demonstration of how nonequivalent control group data can be used in the development field, and because this purpose is best served by a straightforward study, only one impact hypothesis is being examined. The Indonesian rice program was selected as the green revolution activity to be evaluated and the Thailand and Burma cases were selected as nonequivalent control group cases on the basis of those countries use and nonuse (actually very minimal use) of green revolution rice technology and availability of data for the impact variable. It would be highly desirable to have a larger number of both treatment and control group cases. The use of a small number of cases represents an attempt to keep the evaluation from being too unwieldy while still making it possible to illustrate several different nonequivalent control group designs. The use of additional cases would not change the basic evaluation research methodology but would mean that additional analyses of the type reported here would be undertaken. The same would be true if multiple indicators or multiple hypotheses were examined.

The operational procedures used here are fairly straightforward. The use of green revolution technology in Indonesia began in 1968 and continues today. Accordingly, the period prior to 1968 will be considered as the no-treatment era and the period including and following 1968 will be considered as the treatment era. Thailand and Burma are treated as nonequivalent control group cases which did not receive the treatment. Data for the impact variable, annual rice yield in kilograms per hectare, were obtained for the 1961-1973 period for all three countries from the *Production Yearbook* of the Food and Agriculture Organization (FAO) of the United Nations.[9] There may be some error in these data, and their reliability may be somewhat debatable. They do have the virtue of being the best data available, and they were reported to FAO by the policy makers in the three countries.

ʻIt should be noted that this is the type of evaluation research setting where the use of nonequivalent control group data is most appropriate. Experimental designs cannot be employed because randomization was not used to assign cases to treatment and control groups. The use of nonequivalent control group data is possible because the nation-state is the governmental unit associated with the program being evaluated and there are nation-states with and without green revolution programs. Accordingly, designs employing nonequivalent control group data are utilized here. An extended discussion of the plausible rival hypotheses will be presented only for the last design in this chapter. This is done for the sake of brevity. In an actual study only the most powerful feasible design would be used and all of the rival hypotheses would be considered only in light of its use.

One Group Posttest-Only Design

The one group posttest-only design is used as the point of departure for the discussion of the use of the evaluation research methodology to examine the impact hypothesis. It is diagramed in the following manner:

$$X \qquad O$$

where O is the observation or measure of the impact variable and X is the treatment.

When this design is used for the evaluation of the green revolution impact hypothesis, the X is the program initiated in Indonesia in 1968 and O is the Indonesian rice yield in kilograms per hectare for 1968. This information is presented in Figure 3.1. Unfortunately, the impact cannot be examined adequately when this design is employed and none of the plausible rival hypotheses in the internal validity category are controlled.

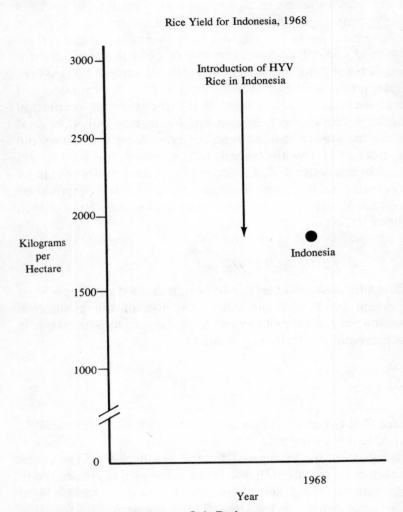

Figure 3.1: One Group Posttest-Only Design

Posttest-Only Design with Nonequivalent Groups

What happens if we also use posttreatment observations for one time period for the impact variable for nonrandomly selected cases which did not receive the treatment? The answer is that we have a posttest-only design with nonequivalent groups:

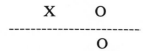

where O is the observation or measure of the impact variable and X is the treatment. This design is an extension of the one group posttest-only design.

When this design is used to evaluate the impact hypothesis, the X is the program initiated in Indonesia in 1968, the O above the broken line is the Indonesian rice yield in kilograms per hectare for 1968, and the O below the broken line is the rice yield in kilograms per hectare for 1968 for a country that had no green revolution rice program. Rice yield data from Thailand are utilized here for the control group case. I felt that the nonequivalent control group case should come from the group of geographically close larger-sized Asian nations. Thailand was the only such country without any reported use of the green revolution technology during 1968.[10] The information for this design for Indonesia and Thailand is reported in Figure 3.2.

As can be seen, the rice yield for Thailand, at 1909 kilograms per hectare for 1968, was actually higher than that for Indonesia, which was 1852 kilograms per hectare for 1968. According to these data, the impact hypothesis should be rejected, and it should be concluded that the Indonesian green revolution program had no impact. Even if the data would have revealed an impact, this design would have convincingly controlled only the history, testing, and statistical regression hypotheses in the internal validity category (because these factors could be expected to affect both Indonesia and Thailand and thus be controlled) and the selection and interactions with selection explanations would definitely not be controlled.[11] Unfortunately, this design, like so many cross-sectional correlational studies found in the social sciences, does not really provide enough information for the results to be convincing because it is not known where the cases stood on the impact variable before the treatment was administered.[12] This pre-experimental design does not allow strong causal inferences and should be used primarily in preliminary studies when a stronger quasi-experimental design is not feasible.

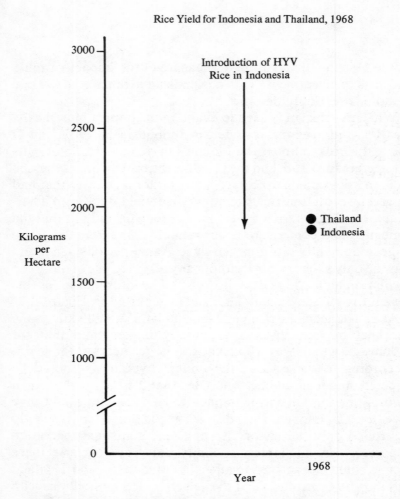

Figure 3.2: Posttest-Only Design with Nonequivalent Groups

Untreated Control Group Design with Pretest and Posttest

What happens when we also use nonrandomly selected pretest observations for one time period for the impact variable for both the treatment and control group cases? In that situation we have an untreated control group design with pretest and posttest:

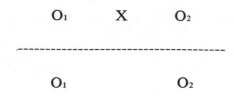

where O is the observation or measure of the impact variable and X is the treatment. This quasi-experimental design can be seen as a combination of the preexperimental, posttest-only design with nonequivalent groups found on the right side of the illustration above, and the preexperimental one group pretest-posttest design, illustrated in the smallpox program study in the last chapter and to be found here in the portion of the illustration above the broken line. It is a stronger design than either of them. It differs from the classic experimental design to be discussed in Chapter 4 in that the two groups have not been equated through the use of randomization.

When this design is used to evaluate the impact hypothesis, the X is the program initiated in Indonesia in 1968, the O_1 above the line is the Indonesian rice yield in kilograms per hectare for 1967, the O_2 above the line is the same information for 1968, the O_1 below the line is the Thailand rice yield in kilograms per hectare for 1967 and the O_2 below the line is the same information for 1968. The information for this design for Indonesia and Thailand is presented in Figure 3.3.

As can be seen, the Indonesian rice yield went up slightly from 1759 kilograms per hectare in 1967 to 1852 kilograms per hectare in 1968. This is the extent of the information that would have been available had the one group pretest-posttest design been used, and it would have been concluded that the green revolution rice program in Indonesia had an impact. However, as can be seen in Figure 3.3, the Thailand rice yield also went up slightly, from 1836 kilograms per hectare in 1967 to 1909 kilograms per hectare in 1968. This finding casts doubt on the prospect that the changed Indonesian program caused the observed Indonesian 1967-1968 increase in rice yield. A nearby country that did not use the green revolution technology

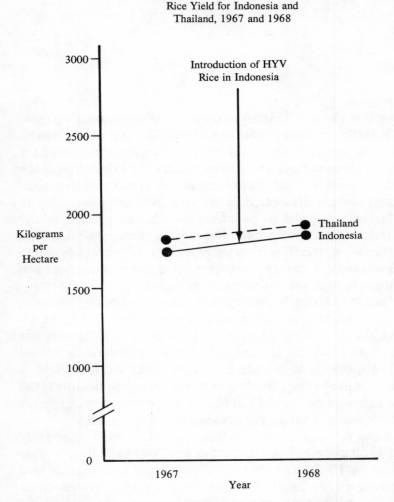

Figure 3.3: Untreated Control Group Design with Pretest and Posttest

showed a similar increase in rice yield. It appears that there were other factors than the green revolution technology at work.

In general, this design controls, at least to a degree, the main effects of history, maturation, selection, testing, and statistical regression because the impact of these factors should have affected both groups, although there would be more faith in this

design if there were numerous cases in both groups. Furthermore, explanations concerning the ambiguity about the direction of causal inference, mortality, diffusion or imitation of
treatment, compensatory equalization of treatment, compensatory rivalry, and resentful demoralization of respondents
receiving less desirable treatments are not threats in this use of
the design. But instrumentation, local history and interaction
with selection explanations are threats here.[13]

Thus the use of this design has cast serious doubt on the
apparent impact of the 1968 change in the Indonesian rice
program. However, this design is most useful when a program
is introduced fully at one time and the effect is of an abrupt
nature and can be observed as a one period change. The 1968
innovation in the Indonesian rice program, as in the case of so
many other complex social action programs in the development field, appears to have taken an extended period of time to
become fully operational and for the impact to be felt. Let us
turn to a nonequivalent control group design which is more
appropriate for the examination of this type of program.

Interrupted Time-Series Design with a Nonequivalent
No-Treatment Control Group Time-Series

When we employ both the strategy of using time-series data
and nonequivalent control group data we have an interrupted
time-series design with a nonequivalent no-treatment control
group time-series:

$$O_1 \quad O_2 \quad O_3 \quad O_4 \quad X \quad O_5 \quad O_6 \quad O_7 \quad O_8$$
$$\text{---}$$
$$O_1 \quad O_2 \quad O_3 \quad O_4 \quad \quad O_5 \quad O_6 \quad O_7 \quad O_8$$

where O is the observation or measure of the impact variable
(the number of data points may vary) and X is the treatment.
This quasi-experimental design has the virtues of the interrupted time-series design, illustrated in the smallpox program
case study in Chapter 2 and to be found here in the portion of
the illustration above the broken line, and adds controls

available through an untreated control group design with pretest and posttest, just illustrated and to be found in the middle of the above illustration. In theory this design is stronger than the interrupted time-series design because it provides a more convincing control of the history explanation.

This is conceptually the strongest of the quasi-experimental designs. It is most powerful when the observed change is of an abrupt nature. But it is well worth undertaking when the expected change is of a longer term, as in this situation. It is probably most useful in the development field when evaluating macroprograms that cover areas where an established indicator system has been in existence for some time, as in this situation. The biggest difficulty in its use is in finding meaningful control group cases without the program change which also meet data requirements. This difficulty presents a serious problem in the evaluation of development activities, both when the nation-state is the unit of analysis and when geographical units within countries are used. This design is strongest when employed in a homogeneous setting where the measurement system and history are identical. In those circumstances a strong control of rival explanations is possible. However, it is also worth undertaking when the measurement system and history are generally similar, as in this case.

When this design is used to evaluate the impact hypothesis, the X is the program initiated in Indonesia in 1968 and the O's above the line represent data on the annual rice yield in kilograms per hectare for Indonesia. The O's below the line represent data points for annual rice yield in kilograms per hectare for the control group cases. Thailand and Burma are used here as control group cases because they are located close to Indonesia and because during the pretreatment period they did not employ the green revolution technology. Furthermore, during the posttreatment period their use of high-yielding rice seeds was low (less than five percent of the national total). They are practically the only such geographically close larger sized Asian countries with such a low percentage of use of high-yielding rice seeds in the posttest era.[14]

Annual data on rice yield in kilograms per hectare for the 1961-1973 era for Indonesia, Thailand and Burma are presented in Figure 3.4. As can be seen, the annual rice yield in Indonesia fluctuated between 1700 and 1800 kilograms per hectare between 1961 and 1967. After the initiation of the use of the green revolution technology in 1968 the yield figures shot upward, reaching almost 2600 kilograms per hectare in 1973.

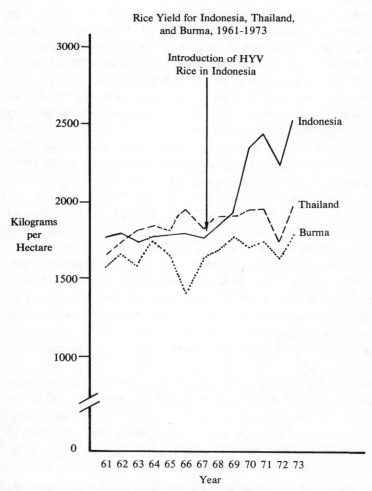

Figure 3.4: Interrupted Time-Series Design with a Nonequivalent No-Treatment Control Group Time-Series

In order to evaluate the impact of the use of green revolution technology in Indonesia, it is necessary to consider what would have happened if the green revolution technology had not been used. It appears highly likely that the trend would have continued as in the past. Under this assumption the Indonesian national rice production is seen as being in equilibrium in regard to yield per hectare, given the old technology. It is, of course, impossible to say what would have happened if the 1968 switch to green revolution technology had not been undertaken. It does seem reasonable to use the extension of the past trend as a benchmark against which to evaluate the effectiveness of the Indonesian green revolution rice program. Furthermore, the control group cases provide information on the extent to which it is legitimate to assume that the past trend would have continued if the green revolution rice technology had not been used.

The years were regressed on the rice yield data to determine the linear trends. The dummy variable strategy of Gujarti[15] was used:

$$Y_t = a + b_1 X_t + b_2 D_t + b_3 (X_t \cdot D_t) + e_t \qquad (3.1)$$

where Y_t equals the rice yield in kilograms per hectare, X_t equals the years, D_t is a dummy variable with O used for the 1961-1967 period and 1 for the 1968-1973 era, a is the intercept, the b's are fixed coefficients, and e is an error term that takes into account factors not otherwise included in the equation. The same statistical assumptions and techniques were used as in the smallpox case study in the previous chapter.

The ordinary least squares technique provided satisfactory estimates (Durbin-Watson d = 2.26) for equation (3.1) for Indonesia.[16] The estimate for the 1961-1967 era indicates that the rice yield trend was relatively stable, increasing at less than one kilogram per hectare per year. The trend line for 1968-1973, the period after the change to the green revolution technology, indicates an average increase in yield of approximately 131 kilograms per hectare per year. Thus the average increase in rice yield per hectare is greater after the intervention with green revolution technology and the difference of approximately 130 kilograms per hectare per year is clearly impressive, as is the overall change in the Indonesian rice yield figures from approximately 1800 to 2600 kilograms per hectare in six years. There is strong empirical support for the impact hypothesis.

Is the change statistically significant? To answer that question the hypothesis that the coefficients describing the 1961-1967 era belong to the same regression as the coefficients describing the 1968-1973 era was examined through use of Chow's F test.[17] The value for the F ratio is 9.47, which is significant beyond the .01 level. Analysis of the t tests for the intercept change and the slope change indicates that both of those changes were significant at the .0001 level.[18] The preintervention and postintervention trends are significantly different from a statistical standpoint.

What about the control group cases? As can be seen in Figure 3.4 the Thailand rice yield fluctuated between a low of approximately 1650 and a high of almost 2000 kilograms per hectare. The ordinary least squares estimates for equation (3.1) for Thailand indicate that the 1961-1967 era trend involved an increase of thirty-six kilograms per hectare per year while the 1968-1973 era trend involved a decrease of three kilograms per hectare per year.[19] The Burma rice yield fluctuated from a low of just under 1500 to a high of just over 1750 kilograms per hectare. The ordinary least squares estimates for equation (3.1) for Burma indicate that the 1961-1967 era trend was a decrease of four kilograms per hectare per year while the 1968-1973 era trend was an increase of four kilograms per hectare per year.[20] Neither of these nonequivalent control group countries displayed the dramatic increase in rice yield during the 1968-1973 period that was found in Indonesia and it is obvious that there were no meaningful substantive improvements in rice yield per hectare in these countries during the 1968-1973 era. Calculation of Chow's F values indicated that in neither country was the 1961-1967 regression line statistically different at the .05 level from the 1968-1973 regression line.[21]

Can the observed results be accounted for by other explanations? In order to answer that question let us consider the plausible rival hypotheses which present challenges to the explanation provided by the impact hypothesis.

It should be recalled that the threat to internal validity casts doubt on whether the hypothesized causal relationship between the operational versions of the variables contained in the impact hypothesis exists in the specific empirical circumstances that are examined.

History. The concern is whether there are other factors (such as an unusually distributed rainfall pattern, the world supply of fertilizer, or the world market price for rice) occurring during the 1968-1973 period which caused the observed change in rice yield. This explanation seems to be controlled in this case because other events occurring during the 1968-1973 era could be expected to affect the rice yield for both the treatment (Indonesia) and control group (Thailand and Burma) cases. In fact, as can be seen in Figure 3.4, that seems to have happened in 1972.

Maturation. The concern here is whether there may have been a maturation process operating in the agricultural field and whether in the course of normal events the rice yield may have increased naturally. This explanation seems to be controlled because one might reasonably expect the maturation trend in Indonesia to be roughly the same during the entire 1961-1973 era. It would appear to be unlikely that the maturation trend for the period before the start of the use of green revolution technology would be too different from the maturation trend after the use of it. Furthermore, if maturation were a major factor, it could be expected to affect the rice yield for both the treatment (Indonesia) and control group (Thailand and Burma) cases.

Testing. In this case the concern is with the effect of publicity regarding a social indicator on later values of that same indicator. Given the nature of the indicator used here, this explanation seems unlikely. It is also unlikely that the testing hypothesis produced the observed 1968-1973 Indonesian rice yield change in that it is not highly probable that the testing effect would suddenly manifest itself in 1968 and produce a sustained impact such as the one revealed here. Furthermore, if testing were a major factor it could be expected to affect the rice yield for Indonesia, Thailand, and Burma.

Instrumentation. Although the data being used in this analysis seem to be the best available, they are, nevertheless, not of the highest quality because of incomplete systems for data collection. It could be that there was an unpublished change in the measurement system which caused the observed increase in Indonesia rice production. Because we would expect any instrumentation alteration to produce an abrupt change which would affect the year in which it is initiated, and because it appears unlikely that there was an alteration in the measurement system every year after the introduction of the green revolution technology which could have produced the sustained increase in Indonesia rice yield, this rival explanation does not seem plausible, except perhaps as an explanation of the rather dramatic increase recorded in Indonesia in 1970. If the data for the treatment (Indonesia) and control group (Thailand and Burma) cases would have been collected by the same system we could have more faith that control group cases actually controlled this rival explanation. Furthermore, had more cases been analyzed we would have even more faith in ruling out this rival explanation because it would be even more unlikely that instrumentation changes would produce an impact in only the treatment cases.

Statistical regression. The possibility exists that the observed Indonesian rice yield change is a statistical artifact because the 1968 revision in the Indonesian rice program was partially a reaction to a perceived failure in the previous program strategy. However, examination of the plot of the Indonesian rice yield data in Figure 3.4 suggests that this plausible rival hypothesis is not likely. Had the 1968 Indonesian rice program change been initiated as a reaction to a crisis rather than to a chronic situation, then the prospect of the observed impact being a statistical artifact would have been greater. Furthermore, the control group cases could be expected to control this plausible explanation. It seems unlikely as a rival explanation.

Selection. It is unlikely that the selection process would produce the observed data pattern, but I would have more faith in ruling out this plausible explanation if I would have used a larger number of cases in both the treatment and control groups. This explanation seems unlikely because the presence of the pretest data series allows the focus to be on the difference in the change in rice yield in the treatment and control group cases, rather than on the difference in the absolute posttest data after the program change in Indonesia.

Mortality. This rival explanation is not plausible here because there was no differential loss of cases for treatment and control groups which could have produced the observed difference between groups.

Interactions with selection. This explanation is concerned with the lack of equivalence in treatment and control group cases and presents a serious challenge to the finding that the 1968 change in the rice program in Indonesia produced the observed change in rice yield. There is some possibility that there is an unidentified difference between Indonesia, on the one hand, and Thailand and Burma, on the other, that produced an interaction with one of the other plausible rival explanations to generate the observed difference in the change in rice yield. I would have more faith in assigning a low probability to this explanation if the number of cases in the treatment and control groups were larger. This explanation is controlled to the extent that if an interaction with selection were at work it could be expected to show up in the 1961-1967 measurements, it is unlikely that it would suddenly manifest itself only in the 1968-1973 era in Indonesia. In this case study I will just have to live with the slight possibility that this explanation is plausible.

Ambiguity about the direction of causal inference. In this study it is possible to tell which variable is the cause and which is the effect because of the time-series nature of the evaluation research design. This explanation it is not a plausible one here.

Diffusion or imitation of the treatment. This explanation is concerned with whether the cases in the control group may have received the treatment through diffusion or imitation and thus whether the treatment may have been eliminated as a possible cause of the difference in impact observed for the groups. In this case the lack of a common communication network and linguistic heterogeneity would seem to rule out this explanation. Even if the information about the details of the green revolution technology would have differed between

the treatment and the control group areas, there is evidence
that the use of high-yielding rice seeds did not spread. This
explanation does not seem plausible in this case.

Compensatory equalization of treatment. The concern
here is whether the treatment may have been given to both the
treatment and control groups, thereby eliminating it as a
possible cause of the difference in impact observed for the
groups. This explanation is plausible especially when the same
authority has responsibility for determining where the treatment is given. In this case completely different sovereign
governments are in control of the countries being studied and
this is a very unlikely rival explanation.

Compensatory rivalry. Did a competitive spirit develop in
the control group and motivate an effort which clouds the real
difference between it and the treatment group on the impact
variable? In some sectors of activity, such as the space race,
national honor may play a major role. However, it seems
unlikely that the peasant farmers of Thailand and Burma were
motivated to match the rice production yield in Indonesia.
Indeed, the data plotted in Figure 3.4 indicate that they did not
do so. This explanation would be more plausible if no difference in the treatment and control groups would have been
revealed.

*Resentful demoralization of respondents receiving less
desirable treatments.* Did the respondents in the control
group become resentful and demoralized because they did not
receive the treatment and did they act in such a way that
created a bias in the observed results? There would not appear
to be a problem in this case because of the physical separation
of the cases in the treatment and control groups, the nature of
the agricultural situation, and the data which indicate a rather
stable rice yield pattern for the control group cases.

Local history. Normally this design would not provide a
very strong control of this rival explanation when only one
treatment case exists. However, the data displayed in Figure
3.4 help rule out this rival explanation. It is somewhat unlikely
that historical experiences unique to Indonesia would suddenly manifest themselves starting in 1968, display the pattern
of sustained growth found in the Indonesian data, and exper-

ience the production dip in 1972 which was also felt by Thailand and Burma. However, in this case we will just have to live with the slight possibility that local history actually provides a plausible explanation for the observed Indonesian rice yield change.

This particular use of the interrupted time-series design with a nonequivalent no-treatment control group time-series has allowed a certain degree of faith in ruling out plausible rival explanations in the internal validity category. These explanations have cast little doubt on the impressive fit of the green revolution impact hypothesis being examined here. This design is an improvement over the untreated control group design with pretest and posttest in that the instrumentation, interactions with selection, and local history explanations in the internal validity category are controlled.

Statistical conclusion validity is concerned with whether the conclusion regarding the impact was a statistical artifact resulting from inappropriate uses of statistical techniques.

Statistical Power. Did the statistical techniques that were used lead to an incorrect conclusion because of small sample size, an inappropriate setting of the level of significance, or the selection of a one-sided hypothesis? In this case the substantive difference conclusion based partly upon a statistical test of significance was the one that there was a difference between the 1961-1967 and the 1968-1973 trends for Indonesia. The size of the sample may present a slight problem. If a larger sample had been available it would have been possible to use Box-Jenkins autoregressive moving average techniques to double-check on the conclusions regarding differences in the pre- and post- 1968 data.[22]

Fishing and the error rate problem. This explanation does not appear to present a problem here because there was no searching through various combinations of cases and variables and there does not seem to be a multiple comparison problem. It appears unlikely that chance could have produced the statistical conclusion regarding impact.

The reliability of measures. There may be a problem in regard to the reliability of measures. The data used are the best available and there is no apparent way to correct for this possible bias. This explanation leaves a question, but based upon the information currently available to me it does not appear to be of sufficient seriousness to warrant the expression of strong reservations regarding the conclusions arrived at in this study.

The reliability of treatment implementation. In this case the lack of standardization of the implementation of the Indonesian rice program would tend to work against the observed impact. This explanation seems irrelevant in this study because only one program is being evaluated and it is being examined in its entirety.

Random irrelevancies in the experimental setting. In this analysis the features of the experimental setting other than the treatment would tend to work against the observed statistical conclusion regarding impact. It is difficult to see how this explanation is plausible here.

Random heterogeneity of respondents. In this study the heterogeneity of respondents with respect to variables that affect the impact variable would tend to work against the observed impact. It would appear to be a plausible explanation had no impact been observed.

This paricular use of the interrupted time-series design with a nonequivalent no-treatment control group time-series has allowed a certain degree of faith in ruling out plausible rival explanations in the statistical conclusion category. The explanations in this category have cast little serious doubt on the impressive fit of the green revolution impact hypothesis being examined.

External validity is concerned with generalizing "across times, settings, and persons."[23] In this study the primary concern of external validity is whether the observed empirical results can be generalized to other time periods or to other countries.

Interaction of treatments and treatments. It could be that the introduction of green revolution technology represents one treatment and that the 1970 managerial revolution represents another treatment and that the same results would not hold in a situation where only one of these treatments is given. Further research is needed on this point.

Interaction of testing and treatment. Is it valid to generalize to situations where the testing is not identical? Because the yield data are available for each year for each country and because they are not highly reactive there would not appear to be too serious a problem in this regard.

Interaction of selection and treatment. Because the concern here is with generalizing to other countries there would not appear to be a problem in regard to this rival explanation. There might be a slight concern regarding the independent variable (the Indonesian rice program) and the use of additional cases would help determine whether there was any special aspect of the Indonesian program which affected the conclusions. Had the concern been in generalizing to other units of analysis, there would have been a problem.

Interaction of setting and treatment. This explanation would appear to present a major problem because the development setting in each country is at least somewhat different from that in any other country. It is not clear to what extent this is a problem and until information is available from other cases it would appear to be wise to be guarded about generalizing to other settings. A partial answer to this question could be obtained by increasing the number of cases examined.

Interaction of history and treatment. There is some chance that this explanation is plausible but on the surface it appears somewhat unlikely that the findings would be time dependent. I do not have serious reservations about generalizing to situations in the past and future.

Generalizing across effect constructs. There appears to be a question about whether the observed impact would hold for other impact variables and constructs. It would not be valid to generalize from the rice yield figures to, for example, health, education, or even wheat impact variables.

Thus there are problems in generalizing the findings to other settings and this should be done with the greatest caution. Had the data examined here been randomly selected from the larger population of countries in the world and had the number of cases been larger, I would have more faith that the explanations in the external validity category were controlled.

Those rival explanations that focus on problems of generalization from operational measures to theoretical constructs are in the construct validity category.

Inadequate preoperational explication of constructs. It would not appear here that inadequate initial clarification of the theoretical constructs led to the development of operational measures which do not adequately represent the construct.

Mono-operation bias. The Indonesian green revolution operationalizations obviously underrepresent the concepts "national green revolution program" and "national increases in agricultural production." It would seem to be important to look at green revolution wheat and corn programs as well as yield figures for other crops. More faith in controlling this rival explanation would have been possible if multiple operationalizations would have been used, as they undoubtedly would have been in an actual study.

Mono-method bias. Did the same method for giving treatments and/or collecting data on responses result in a bias in regard to the construct? It is difficult to see how the nationwide green revolution rice program in Indonesia, which extended over several years, was systematically biased in this regard.

Hypothesis-guessing within experimental conditions. It seems unlikely that knowledge of the hypothesis could lead to the observed impact. Knowledge of the hypothesis without the green revolution technology would seem to be inadequate. This explanation does not seem plausible.

Evaluation apprehension. Were the subjects apprehensive about being evaluated and did they, therefore, bias their reported attitudes and behavior? Given the nature of the rice programs it is difficult to see how this question is of great relevance. This explanation does seem plausible to the extent that some of the rice yield data represent the peasants' subjective estimates of their own rice production. It is, therefore, not ruled out but would not seem to be highly plausible.

Experimenter expectancies. Was the observed impact the result of a data collection bias resulting from the hopes and expectations of the experimenter? There may be a bias of this sort in this study. The governmental officials ultimately responsible for the data had a vested interest in seeing the massive and expensive social action program be a success. It is possible that some bias entered into the reported data. Independent audits of the data collection process might have revealed the extent, if any, to which this is a problem if they had been conducted when the data were collected.

Confounding levels of constructs and constructs. Did operational procedures cover the full range of possible values for the variables and thus miss part of the relationship between them? There would not seem to be a problem in this study in regard to the impact variable. There could be a problem with the independent variable. While it seems clear that the Indonesian green revolution rice program had an impact on rice yield per hectare, it would appear to be questionable to assume that a green revolution program that is quite different in nature would have the same impact.

Generalizing across time. It would not seem to be valid to generalize from the impact observed using the operational measures to the conclusion that the impact holds across time for the theoretical construct because it is well known that the green revolution technology is good only for one growing season. There is no reason for generalizing the impact beyond that time period.

Interaction of procedure and treatment. It does not appear that the operational procedures allowed the respondents to gain information which created a bias in the observed results. Information without the green revolution seeds and fertilizer could not have produced the observed impact.

There is a problem in generalizing from the observed empirical results to the theoretical constructs in the green revolution impact hypothesis. Construct validity is a problem.

It has been demonstrated that there was a substantial increase in rice yield in Indonesia after the introduction of the green revolution rice technology and that a similar increase in rice yield did not occur in Thailand and Burma, where the green revolution rice technology was not used widely. After consideration of the rival explanations in the internal validity and statistical conclusion categories there appears to be no highly plausible rival explanation for the observed impact. It is reasonable to conclude that the Indonesian green revolution rice program had a significant impact on rice yield in Indonesia.

However, consideration of the explanations in the external validity and construct validity categories suggests that there are problems in generalizing the observed results to other countries and in generalizing the operationalizations to the constructs contained in the impact hypothesis. I, consequently, am left with considerable doubt regarding the adequacy of the test of the impact hypothesis stated earlier in the chapter. Clearly, the use of ideas such as multiple operationalization would have improved the control of rival explanations in the construct validity category, and the use of a larger number of cases and heterogeneous groups of countries, settings, and places would have improved the control of rival explanations in the external validity category.

Summary and Conclusions

The case study of the Indonesian rice program has presented a demonstration of how nonequivalent control group data can be of assistance in ruling out rival explanations in impact studies of development activities. A researcher can move from evaluation research designs employing a single impact variable data point to those employing nonequivalent control group data and time-series data. Doing so, of course, improves the strength of evaluation research studies by allowing for a more adequate test of the impact hypothesis and a more adequate control of plausible rival hypotheses. Unfortunately, it is not possible to offer advice in simple terms on how to seek out the nonequivalent control group cases, and there is no single design using nonequivalent control group data that is best for all circumstances.

Unfortunately, evaluation research designs employing nonequivalent control group data are not without problems. As in the case of other evaluation research designs there are potential applied research problems concerning the formulation of meaningful impact hypotheses, measurement concerns, organizational resistances, data availability, and data analysis, and there are potential research utilization problems concerning factors such as the timing and relevance of studies. Furthermore, there is a real danger in being misled seriously by designs using nonequivalent control group data. This happens when the nonequivalent control group cases are so different that they confuse rather than clarify the impact of the intervention and actually lead to incorrect conclusions. This has happened frequently enough that Donald T. Campbell and Robert F. Boruch recently published an extensive cautionary statement regarding the use of designs employing nonequivalent control group data.[24] An evaluation researcher obviously must have a good substantive knowledge of a problem and needs to exercise extreme care when utilizing nonequivalent control group data. Whenever possible it is better to use randomization to create experimental designs with equivalent groups. Let us turn now to a consideration of that type of design.

NOTES

1. For an overview of the Indonesian rice program, see Gary E. Hansen, "Indonesia's green revolution: the abandonment of a non-market strategy towards change," *Seadag Papers on Problems of Development in Southeast Asia,* mimeo, New York, Southeast Asia Development Advisory Group, circa 1972; and Richard W. Franke, "The green revolution in a Javanese village," unpublished Ph.D. Thesis, Harvard University, 1972.

2. In addition to the Indonesian government the following organizations have been involved in the Indonesian green revolution rice program: United States Agency for International Development, Ford Foundation, Agricultural Development Council, International Rice Research Institute, Food and Agriculture Organization of the United Nations, and several multinational corporations.

3. Franke, "The green revolution": 29-47.

4. Franke, ibid.: 47.

5. Hansen, "Indonesia's green revolution": 17.

6. For an introduction to the green revolution technology, see Dana G. Dalrymple, *Development and Spread of High-Yielding Varieties of Wheat and Rice in the Less Developed Nations* (Washington, D.C.: United States Department of Agriculture, 1974).

7. For a concise treatment of the social aspects of the green revolution, see Lester R. Brown, "The social impact of the green revolution," *International Conciliation* 581 (1971): 5-45.

8. I used the per hectare figures in order to control for changes in the amount of land used for rice production and therefore to isolate the actual effect of the green revolution technology on rice yield.

9. *Production Yearbook* (Rome: Food and Agriculture Organization, annually). The use of the 1961-1973 time period was based on the following considerations: (1) the rice yield data do not seem comparable before and after 1961; and (2) after 1973 the use of green revolution technology was too widespread in the nonequivalent control group cases.

10. Information on the percentage of use of high-yielding varieties of rice in various countries was obtained from Dalrymple, *Development and Spread of High-Yielding Varieties:* 72. The high-yielding rice seeds were introduced in Thailand in 1969.

11. The instrumentation hypothesis is not controlled automatically in this situation because the data collection system is different for the two countries. The mortality, diffusion or imitation of the treatment, compensatory equalization of treatment, and compensatory rivalry hypotheses in the internal validity category seem unlikely in this situation.

12. This design is the equivalent of the cross-sectional correlation design used so frequently in the development field. It can be written in the following single equation form:

$$Y = a + bX + e$$

where Y is the dependent variable (in this case the impact variable), X is the independent variable (in this case a dummy variable representing the treatment and its lack), a is the intercept, b is a fixed coefficient, and e is an error term that takes into account factors not otherwise included in the equation. Changing the scale of the independent variable to the ordinal or interval level, simply changing the number of cases from two to 150 countries, or adding other independent variables would not change the basic design, although the increase in the number of cases might allow us to discount somewhat the seriousness of the threat presented by certain plausible rival hypotheses. I do feel that the deduction of the impact hypothesis from a theory and the absence of theoretically based alternative impact hypotheses would make the use of this design more meaningful. I would emphasize that there is a role for a study that generates correlational evidence. Correlation is a necessary but not sufficient condition for causation and this design may be especially useful for the generation of causal impact hypotheses.

13. The instrumentation hypothesis is not controlled in this situation because the data collection system is different for the two countries.

14. Dalrymple, *Development and Spread of High-Yielding Varieties:* 72.

15. Damodar Gujarti, "Use of dummy variables in testing equality between sets of coefficients in two linear regressions: a note," *The American Statistician* 24,4(1970): 50-52; and Damodar Gujarti, "Use of dummy variables in testing for equality between sets of coefficients in linear regressions: a generalization," *The American Statistician* 24,5(1970): 18-22.

16. Most of the statistical analyses in this chapter were done on the IBM 370 computer at the University of Southern California. The Statistical Analysis System was used for the calculation of everything except the values for Chow's F test, which I calculated by hand. I am grateful to Robert E. Bowen for doing the computer analyses for me.

The annual rice yield data in kilograms per hectare for Indonesia for 1961-1973 are as follows: 1762, 1786, 1723, 1763, 1771, 1775, 1759, 1852, 1941, 2361, 2410, 2258, and 2564.

The following ordinary least squares estimates were obtained for equation (3.1) for Indonesia:

$$a = 570 \ (.02)* \qquad\qquad R^2 = .91$$
$$b_1 = 0.61 \ (.03)* \qquad\quad\ F = 32.23**$$
$$b_2 = -255{,}067 \ (-4.17)** \quad \text{D-W d} = 2.26*$$
$$b_3 = 129.68 \ (4.17)**$$

where the t tests for the regression coefficients are in parentheses and * indicates no significance at the .01 level and ** indicates significance at the .0001 level.

17. G.C. Chow, "Tests of equality between coefficients in two linear regressions," *Econometrica* 28 (1960): 591-605. The use of Chow's test in this circumstance involves regressing the years on the rice yield data for Indonesia and comparing the results with those obtained when equation (3.1) is used.

The following ordinary least squares estimates were obtained for the regression of the years on the rice yield data for Indonesia:

$$a = -129{,}129 \ (-5.45)** \qquad R^2 = .74$$
$$b = 66.65 \ (5.53)** \qquad\qquad\ F = 30.61**$$
$$\qquad\qquad\qquad\qquad\qquad\qquad \text{D-W d} = .91*$$

where the t tests for the regression coefficients are in parentheses and * indicates significance at the .01 level and ** indicates significance at the .0002 level. Because of positively autocorrelated error terms the R^2, F and t values are inflated and should not be relied upon.

An analysis of the autocorrelation of error terms suggests that the Indonesian green revolution rice program had an impact. When the years are regressed on the rice yield data, the Durbin-Watson d of .91 suggests first order autocorrelation of error terms at the .01 level and thus an incorrect specification of the model. When the intervention model represented by equation (3.1) is analyzed, the Durbin-Watson d of 2.26 does not suggest first order autocorrelation of error terms at the .01 level and an incorrect specification of the model.

As noted in the text, the value for Chow's F is 9.47, which is significant beyond the .01 level. The fact that the significant autocorrelation of error terms is positive in the first case mentioned in the paragraph above suggests that the unexplained sum of squares is underestimated in that case and hence that the value of Chow's F is underestimated. In this situation the F value is significant and it does not really matter. I did not use generalized least squares (GLS) estimation procedures because of the difficulties in comparing GLS variance estimates with other GLS variance estimates or with those obtained using ordinary least squares techniques. My assessment of the impact of the Indonesian rice program is not tied exclusively to the use of Chow's F test and an unbiased estimate of it.

18. See note 16 for the details. Incidently, examination of the plot of Indonesian data in Figure 3.4 indicates that the biggest increase in rice yield per hectare took place in 1970. It appears that the 1970 managerial revolution had a significant impact. This is a matter that undoubtedly would be explored further in an actual study. I am grateful to Brian Flay for reminding me to point this out.

19. The annual rice yield data in kilograms per hectare for Thailand for 1961-1973 are as follows: 1658, 1720, 1808, 1838, 1781, 1977, 1836, 1909, 1934, 1973, 1992, 1776, and 1982.

The following ordinary least squares estimates were obtained for equation (3.1) for Thailand:

$$a = -69,813 \ (-2.38)** \qquad R^2 = .61$$
$$b_1 = 36.46 \ (2.44)** \qquad F = 4.69**$$
$$b_2 = 76,808 \ (1.62)** \qquad \text{D-W } d = 2.91*$$
$$b_3 = -39.04 \ (-1.62)**$$

where the t tests for the regression coefficients are in parentheses and * indicates significance at the .01 level and ** indicates no significance at the .01 level. Because of negatively autocorrelated error terms the R^2, F and t values are biased downward and should not be relied upon.

The following ordinary least squares estimates were obtained for the regression of the years on the rice yield data for Thailand:

$$a = -37,080 \ (-3.13)* \qquad R^2 = .49$$
$$b = 19.80 \ (3.28)* \qquad F = 10.78*$$
$$\qquad\qquad\qquad\qquad \text{D-W } d = 2.24**$$

where the t tests for the regression coefficients are in parentheses and * indicates significance at the .01 level and ** indicates no significance at the .01 level.

An analysis of the autocorrelation of error terms suggests that the 1961-1967 era is not significantly different from the 1968-1973 era in Thailand. When the years are regressed on the rice yield data, the Durbin-Watson d of 2.24 does not suggest first order autocorrelation of error terms at the .01 level and an incorrect specification of the model. When the change model represented by equation (3.1) is analyzed, the Durbin-Watson d of 2.91 suggests first order autocorrelation of error terms at the .01 level and an incorrect specification of the model.

The value for the Chow F test is 1.33, which is not significant at the .05 level. The fact that the significant autocorrelation of error terms is negative in the second case discussed in the paragraph above suggests that the unexplained sum of squares is overestimated in that case and hence that the value of Chow's F is underestimated. See note 17 for the reasoning as to why generalized least squares techniques were not used to recalculate Chow's F test. My assessment of the change in the Thailand trend is not tied exclusively to the use of Chow's F and an unbiased estimate of it.

20. The annual rice yield data in kilograms per hectare for Burma for 1961-1973 are as follows: 1588, 1648, 1597, 1710, 1661, 1469, 1651, 1684, 1709, 1697, 1716, 1626, and 1757.

The following ordinary least squares estimates were obtained for equation (3.1) for Burma:

$$a = 8,983 \ (0.34)** \qquad R^2 = .33$$
$$b_1 = -3.75 \ (-0.28)** \qquad F = 1.46**$$
$$b_2 = -14,885 \ (-0.35)** \qquad \text{D-W } d = 2.70*$$
$$b_3 = 7.61 \ (0.36)**$$

where the t tests for the regression coefficients are in parentheses and * indicates significance at the .01 level and ** indicates no significance at the .01 level. Because of negatively autocorrelated error terms the R^2, F and t values are biased downward and should not be relied upon.

The following ordinary least squares estimates were obtained for the regression of the years on the rice yield for Burma:

$$a = -16,199 \ (-1.63)^* \qquad R^2 = .23$$
$$b = 9.10 \ (1.80)^* \qquad F = 3.23^*$$
$$\text{D-W } d = 2.29^*$$

where the t tests for the regression coefficients are in parentheses and * indicates no significance at the .01 level.

An analysis of the autocorrelation of error terms suggests that the 1961-1967 era is not meaningfully different from the 1968-1973 era in Burma. When the years are regressed on the rice yield data, the Durbin-Watson d of 2.29 does not suggest first order autocorrelation of error terms at the .01 level and an incorrect specification of the model. When the change model represented by equation (3.1) is analyzed, the Durbin-Watson d of 2.70 suggests first order autocorrelation of error terms at the .01 level and an incorrect specification of the model.

The value for the Chow F test is 0.66, which is not significant at the .05 level. The fact that the significant autocorrelation of error terms is negative in the second case discussed in the paragraph above suggests that the unexplained sum of squares is overestimated in that case and hence that the value of Chow's F is underestimated. See note 17 for the reasoning as to why generalized least squares techniques were not used to recalculate the value of Chow's F test. My assessment of the change in the Burma trend is not tied exclusively to the use of Chow's F and an unbiased estimate of it.

21. The details of the Chow's F test for Thailand and Burma are presented in notes 19 and 20. Estimation problems mean that those estimates are biased and cannot be relied upon.

22. Thomas D. Cook and Donald T. Campbell, "The design and conduct of quasi-experiments and true experiments in field settings," in M. D. Dunnette, ed., *Handbook of Industrial and Organizational Psychology* (Chicago: Rand McNally, 1976): 275. Note that fifty cases should be available for use of Box-Jenkins techniques, and unfortunately, only thirteen cases are available for use here. My thinking here is similar to that presented in note 16 of Chapter 2, although in this case the fact that there are only thirteen cases probably means that nothing can be done with the Box-Jenkins techniques.

23. Cook and Campbell, ibid.: 234.

24. Donald T. Campbell and Robert F. Boruch, "Making the case for randomized assignment to treatments by considering the alternatives: six ways in which quasi-experimental evaluations in compensatory education tend to underestimate effects," in Carl A. Bennett and Arthur A. Lumsdaine, eds., *Evaluation and Experiment: Some Critical Issues in Assessing Social Programs* (New York: Academic Press, 1975): 195-296.

Chapter 4

USING RANDOMIZATION

The best method for controlling rival explanations in the internal validity category involves the random assignment of cases to treatment and control groups. When this is done, there is a true experiment. In this chapter, information on the Mexican televised learning program Plaza Sesamo is used to demonstrate how a randomized experimental design can be employed to control rival explanations. It is worth noting that the study reported in this chapter was planned before the treatment was given, instead of retrospectively as were the studies presented in Chapters 2 and 3. This resulted in an evaluation which used a stronger design and is in general superior to the earlier ones.

Plaza Sesamo

Education appears to be one of the key factors in the development process, and considerable effort has been devoted to educational activities, such as teacher training, curriculum development, and literacy programs in developing countries. The general success of Sesame Street in the United States during the late 1960s appeared to open up new possibilities for preschool education by television, and the original Sesame Street programs were translated into numerous languages and distributed in various developing countries. In Mexico a "completely new [Sesame Street] production adapted to Mexican Culture"[1] was developed in 1971. It was called Plaza Sesamo. The program presented the possibility of dramatic increases in preschool learning for those watching it.

Evaluation Research Considerations

A complex randomized experiment to evaluate the impact of Plaza Sesamo was designed by researchers associated with the Centro de Investigaciones Psicopedagogicas, Asociacion Civil (CIPAC) in Mexico City. Rogelio Diaz-Guerrero and Wayne H. Holtzman summarized the experiment in the following manner:

> A total of 221 children from three different lowest-class day care centers, equally divided by ages 3, 4, and 5, and by sex were randomly assigned to experimental and control groups. Complete data were later obtained for 173 of these children. A battery of nine tests . . . [was] individually administered pre-, during and posttelecast. Measures of attention to the program and of attendance were also taken.[2]

Children in the experimental groups viewed Plaza Sesamo programs for fifty minute periods during each weekday. It took six months to complete the entire series of 150 programs. During the time when the children in the experimental group were watching Plaza Sesamo, those in the control group were viewing "cartoons and other noneducational TV programs in a separate room."[3] The same tests were given during the same general time to those in both the experimental and control groups on a random basis, but the sample of participants was not drawn randomly from a larger universe.

Only one impact hypothesis will be examined here: The Plaza Sesamo television program resulted in an increase in general knowledge for those in the Centro de Investigaciones Psicopedagogicas experiment who viewed the program. A complete systematic evaluation of the Plaza Sesamo program would focus on various aspects of the program and a multiplicity of impact variables would be used to represent program goals and possible side effects. The examination of multiple hypotheses would mean that numerous analyses such as this one would be conducted.

The operationalizations and data used by researchers associated with the Plaza Sesamo experiment are utilized in this illustration to examine the impact hypothesis. The independent variable is the Plaza Sesamo television program. Those viewing the program are in the experimental group and those not viewing the program are in the control group. The data for the dependent variable are those collected for the general knowledge test. Diaz-Guerrero and Holtzman noted:

> This test contains 37 items yielding a possible range of scores from 0 to 37. Items consist of questions such as "What do we smell with?" "What do we see with?" "What is the name of different parts of the body?" and "Which one of these four objects is the heaviest?"[4]

The test was administered individually to each child in the experiment by "carefully trained preschool teachers and psychological assistants."[5] The basis for the discussion of rival explanations that is presented here is the article by Diaz-Guerrero and Holtzman that appeared in the *Journal of Educational Psychology*.[6]

It is worth noting in passing that multiple impact variables were used in the Plaza Sesamo evaluation. Among the indicators employed were the following: general knowledge, numbers, relations, embedded figures, parts of the whole, ability to sort, letters and words, classification skills, and oral comprehension. Tests to measure individual scores for these variables were given to those in both the experimental and control groups at three points in time: (a) immediately prior to the exposure to Plaza Sesamo or the control films; (b) seven weeks later; and (c) six months later at the end of the experiment.[7] Attendance records were carefully kept for those in the experimental and control groups. Those in the experimental group were also rated by trained observers in regard to the degree of attention exhibited to the program being shown. Each individual was identified according to group (experimental or control), sex, and age.

Pretest-Posttest Control Group Design

The pretest-posttest control group design is the classical experimental design:

$$O_1 \quad X \quad O_2$$

$$O_1 \qquad O_2$$

where O is the observation or measure of the impact variable and X is the treatment. If the treatment had any impact, there should be a difference in the change observed for the groups. This design differs from the untreated control group design with pretest and posttest in that here the groups have been equated through the use of randomization. Many of the rival explanations in the internal validity category are ruled out by the process of randomization.

In this illustration we are concerned with a field experiment. The Plaza Sesamo program is the X; the O_1 is the general knowledge test given to all children immediately before the series of 150 television programs; and the O_2 is the general knowledge test given six months later at the end of the series of programs. The relevant information is presented in Figure 4.1.

As can be seen, there is a posttest difference in the means for the general knowledge scores for the experimental and control groups. The pretest mean score for the experimental group is fourteen and the posttest mean score for the group is twenty-four. The pretest mean score for the control group is fourteen and the posttest mean score is nineteen. Thus the posttest difference in means for the groups is five. There is empirical support for the impact hypothesis. However, while some individuals may consider the posttest difference of five to have substantive significance, others might not. Is the difference statistically significant? Diaz-Guerrero and Holtzman conducted an analysis of covariance of these data and reported that the difference is significant at the .001 level.[8]

The threat to internal validity casts doubt on whether the hypothesized causal relationship between operational versions of the variables specified in the impact hypothesis actually exists in the specific circumstances that are examined.

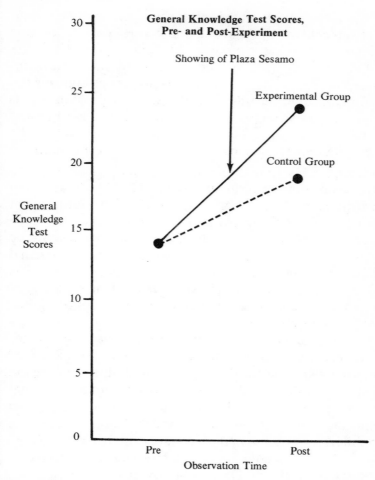

**General Knowledge Test Scores,
Pre- and Post-Experiment**

Showing of Plaza Sesamo

Experimental Group

Control Group

General
Knowledge
Test
Scores

Pre   Post
Observation Time

Figure 4.1: Pretest-Posttest Control Group Design,

In this situation the threat relates to whether the Plaza Sesamo program actually caused the difference in the observed increase in scores on the general knowledge test. The pretest-posttest control group design, which utilizes random assignment to experimental and control groups and pre- and post-test observations, eliminates eight possible rival explanations in the internal validity category in the circumstances discussed here. The pretest-posttest nature of the design controls ambiguity about the direction of causal inference. The random assignment of subjects to experimental and control groups controls the selection and interactions with selection explanations. The lack of change in testing procedures controls the instrumentation explanation. The use of equivalent groups controls the history, maturation, testing, and statistical regression explanations in that these factors could be expected to have an equal effect on both groups. The remaining explanations in the internal validity category need to be considered in detail.

Mortality. This rival explanation seems plausible on the surface because the experiment began with 231 children and ended with only 173 children. The details of this loss are not presented by Diaz-Guerrero and Holtzman. They do argue however that "No discernible bias due to dropouts could be discovered."[9] This rival explanation would not be a problem if further checking revealed that their conclusion is correct.

Diffusion or imitation of the treatment. This rival explanation would be plausible if the children in the control group viewed Plaza Sesamo. Great care was taken by the researchers to prevent this from happening. Plaza Sesamo was shown twice daily in Mexico City during the experimental period. The 3:00 pm showing was used for the experiment, and the children in the control group were shown other television programs at that time. To prevent the children in the control group from watching the 6:00 pm showing on another channel, the control group children were kept in the day care centers until 7:00 pm, and they engaged in noncognitive games and social activities from 6:00 until 7:00 pm. During the course of the experiment the number of daily absences averaged twenty-four for the entire group of 173 children. This amounts to an absence rate of 14 percent. A special study indicated that 50 percent of the experimental children and 34 percent of the control children watched Plaza Sesamo when absent due to sickness,[10] thus we can estimate that between four and five percent of the control group watched Plaza Sesamo on an average day. Taking into account the turnover in absent students, it would appear that only a very slight bias would have been introduced because of diffusion of the treatment during absences. Furthermore, the day care centers were kept open during the vacations in order to prevent control group children from watching Plaza Sesamo during the holiday periods. The attendance record during one long vacation was the highest for the entire six months of the experiment because the principal investigator for the experiment donated his personal color television set to be raffled off among the parents of children with perfect attendance during the vacation. It appears that there was no special diffusion of treatment during vacation periods. This rival explanation does not seem plausible because of the care and good sense employed by the researchers.

Compensatory equalization of treatment. Was the treatment given to both the treatment and control groups, thereby eliminating it as a possible cause of the difference in impact observed for the groups? It should be clear from the above discussion that this did not happen.

Compensatory rivalry. Did a competitive spirit develop in the control group and motivate an effort which clouds the real difference between it and the treatment group on the impact variable? Even if the children in the control group had been motivated to such an effort, it is doubtful that they could have achieved an increase in the general knowledge test scores on their own. Furthermore, this rival explanation would seem more plausible if no difference would have been observed in the two groups.

Resentful demoralization of respondents receiving less desirable treatments. Did respondents in the control group become resentful and demoralized because they did not receive the treatment and did they act in such a way that created a bias in the observed results? There is no evidence that this situation developed in the Plaza Sesamo experiment, although more faith in ruling out this explanation would have been possible if Diaz-Guerrero and Holtzman would have addressed this concern explicitly.

Local history. This rival explanation suggests that the "different treatments . . . [may] be associated with all the unique historical experiences that each group has"[11] and the treatment may not be responsible for the observed difference between groups. Diaz-Guerrero and Holtzman did address this concern:

> Two minor exceptions to the general rule that experimental and control children were treated alike had to be made because of the space limitations within the day care centers. The experimental groups saw "Plaza Sesamo" in groups averaging in size about 15 children, while the control groups viewed cartoons in groups approximately twice this size. This type of distribution might favor slightly the experimental cases in any comparisons, although in both experimental and control groups there was no difficulty in viewing the television screen. The second difference between the experimental and control groups arose from the fact that the control cases were kept in the day-care centers until 7 o'clock in the evening while the experimentals were released shortly after 5 o'clock.[12]

Diaz-Guerrero and Holtzman view the bias because of these factors as being minor. It appears that this rival explanation is ruled out.

After consideration of the relevant rival explanations in the internal validity category, it appears that there is no highly plausible rival explanation for the observed impact.

Statistical conclusion validity is concerned with whether the conclusion regarding the impact was a statistical artifact resulting from inappropriate uses of statistical techniques. In this circumstance the concern is whether the observed difference in groups is truly significant from a statistical standpoint.

Statistical power. In the Plaza Sesamo experiment the sample size was an adequate 173, the difference of five in the mean posttest scores was significant at the .001 level (most researchers would consider this an appropriate level of significance), and the impact hypothesis does not appear to be one-sided.[13] It does not seem likely that the statistical techniques produced an incorrect conclusion.

Fishing and the error rate problem. No searching for significant differences was done in this evaluation research study. It does not seem plausible that chance produced the statistical conclusion regarding impact.

The reliability of measures. Because Diaz-Guerrero and Holtzman report a pre- and post-correlation of r = .78 for the general knowledge test, it appears that the measure utilized here is reasonably reliable.[14] It seems unlikely that measures of low reliability produced the statistical conclusion regarding impact.

The reliability of treatment implementation. The reliability of the treatment implementation appears to present no problem here because the Plaza Sesamo program was on tape and it was viewed by those in the experimental group at the same time on the same television channel.

Random irrelevancies in the experimental setting. It would be expected in this situation that random irrelevancies in the experimental setting would effect both experimental and control groups and that they would occur infrequently over a six month period and have little impact. This rival explanation does not seem highly plausible because of the extended period of the experiment and the tight controls that were exercised by the researchers.

Random heterogeneity of respondents. One plausible heterogeneity factor in this circumstance would appear to be age. If the children were too young, they might not be able to absorb the large amount of information given by Plaza Sesamo and the impact on the general knowledge score might be minimal. On the other hand, if the children were too old, they might already have acquired the information given by Plaza Sesamo and the impact on the general knowledge score might be minimal. If the age span was too great, the difference between groups might be minimal. Diaz-Guerrero and Holtzman did control for age and estimate its impact. Whereas the overall general knowledge score difference between experimentals and controls was 5.0, the difference for three year olds was 2.7, the difference for four year olds was 7.3, and the difference for five year olds was 4.8.[15] It appears that the heterogeneity of ages had an impact on the aggregated results of the test of the impact hypothesis. The impact was not, however, of sufficient size to be of serious concern. This rival explanation would appear to be more relevant had no impact been observed. In that circumstance the concern would be whether the heterogeneity of respondents caused the lack of a statistically significant difference in groups.

None of the rival explanations in the statistical conclusion validity category seems to be highly plausible and no serious doubt has been cast on the conclusions arrived at through the use of statistical tests of significance.

External validity focuses on whether the observed results of an evaluation research study can be expected to be the same at a later time, such as next year, in a different setting, such as another country, or when other persons are involved. The relevance of these concerns for the making of decisions on when, where, and to whom to show the Plaza Sesamo program appear to be obvious.

Interaction of treatments and treatments. The results of this evaluation should not be generalized automatically to other times, settings, or persons if the treatment is altered significantly. For example, it could be the case that showing only the last three months of the Plaza Sesamo series would produce the same results or completely different results. If the treatment is altered significantly then the impact should be evaluated once again.

Interaction of testing and treatment. These results should be accepted as valid only for the Plaza Sesamo series actually shown and for the particular general knowledge test utilized in the experiment. The impact of Plaza Sesamo in regard to another operationalization of general knowledge would need to be evaluated systematically.

Interaction of selection and treatment. It would appear to be problematical to generalize the observed results to other categories of subjects (e.g., other age groups, other social classes, those outside the Mexican culture, those in non-Spanish speaking countries). More faith would be had in generalizing to children in the same category as those utilized in this study if the subjects for the study would have been selected from the larger population on a random basis. Additional evidence would seem to be needed before the observed results are generalized to situations where the categories of respondents are not identical. On the surface it would appear to be reasonable to generalize to other respondents in the same category as those studied here.

Interaction of setting and treatment. The setting for this experiment involved a group of children in day care centers. It would be best to check the impact once again if a significantly different setting is used (e.g., larger or smaller groups or situations where individual children watch Plaza Sesamo).

Interaction of history and treatment. Is it valid to generalize to situations in the past and future because they are not identical? This question would not seem to present serious problems if the time period of interest is not too far removed. If is is quite different, say several years, perhaps the impact should be checked again.

Generalizing across effect constructs. It may not be possible to generalize the impact of Plaza Sesamo in regard to constructs other than general knowledge. If one wanted to generalize to other constructs it would be necessary to operationalize them. The researchers associated with the Centro de Investigaciones Psycopedagogicas' evaluation of Plaza Sesamo measured the impact on eight other tests which represent other constructs. That work obviously would need to be consulted before anything could be said about the impact of Plaza Sesamo in regard to those constructs.

Consideration of the rival explanations in the external validity category suggests that there are problems in generalizing the observed results to other times, settings and persons. It would appear, however, that careful generalization to modal and target instances might be possible.

The rival explanations that focus on problems of generalization from operational measures to theoretical constructs are in the construct validity category. The first thing to note is that the independent variable in the impact hypothesis is the Plaza Sesamo television program. It has not been argued that this variable represents an abstract concept and no attempt will be made to generalize to a construct such as televised learning programs. The dependent variable in the impact hypothesis is general knowledge and it is of interest to examine whether the test that was employed represents adequately the construct of general knowledge.

Inadequate preoperational explication of constructs. The question is whether the lack of initial clarification of this construct could mean that the general knowledge test that was used does not represent adequately the construct. Diaz-Guerrero and Holtzman do not develop in their article in the *Journal of Educational Psychology*[16] the concept of general knowledge and hence it is difficult to evaluate whether the general knowledge test, which they do not present in detail, represents adequately the construct of general knowledge. It should be noted that Diaz-Guerrero and Holtzman treat this test as one of three "Content-Achievement Tests."[17] Unfortunately, they do not develop the construct of content-achievement and it is difficult to tell whether the three tests represent adequately this construct. Diaz-Guerrero and Holtzman appear to use the general knowledge test as one of eight measures for the construct of learning.[18] Unfortunately, this construct is not clarified in their article, and it is difficult to evaluate the adequacy of any of the tests as measures of learning. More checking is needed in regard to this plausible rival hypothesis. It is not ruled out as a result of the information currently available.

Mono-operation bias. It could be that the construct of general knowledge is underrepresented or its measurement contains irrelevancies because only one general knowledge test was used. It would appear to be less of a problem in regard to constructs when multiple operationalizations are used.

Mono-method bias. The major concern here would be in regard to collection of data for the impact variable. The test was administered individually by examiners. It could be that if another method were used that the results would be different and the generalization to the construct would be different. It is, however, difficult to conceive of another method that could be used with three to five year olds.

Hypothesis-guessing within experimental conditions. It seems unlikely that three to five year olds would have guessed the impact hypothesis and compensated without assistance for the knowledge obtained by the experimental subjects, and thus have created a bias in the test of the impact hypothesis.

Evaluation apprehension. Were subjects apprehensive

about being evaluated and, therefore, did they bias their reported attitudes or behavior? Given the nature of the Plaza Sesamo experiment, the treatment, and the test used, it is difficult to see how this concern is of great relevance, although it cannot be ruled out completely.

Experimenter expectancies. Was the observed impact the result of a data collection bias resulting from the hopes and expectations of the experimenter? This possibility is a concern here because the tests were administered individually and because Diaz-Guerrero and Holtzman do not discuss any controls for this rival explanation. This concern must be considered to be problematical until information is obtained which rules it out. The use of a double blind experiment would normally be used to control this plausible rival hypothesis, but it is difficult to conceive how such a procedure could be used in this case.

Confounding levels of constructs and constructs. The concern here is whether the full range of possible values for the construct of general knowledge was captured and thus whether the relationship between Plaza Sesamo and general knowledge is correctly estimated. It is not possible for me to rule out this concern because Diaz-Guerrero and Holtzman are not explicit about measurement matters in their article.

Generalizing across time. It could be that the impact that was observed was only of a short-term nature and that if the same tests were given one year later that no differences would be observed between the experimental and control groups. It would be best not to consider the impact as a long-term one without further evidence.

Interaction of procedure and treatment. Did the operational procedures allow the respondents to gain information which created a bias in the observed results? Additional information is needed on the operational procedures before this rival explanation can be ruled out.

Consideration of the rival explanations in the construct validity category suggests that great care should be taken in attempting to generalize the results of this evaluation research study across treatments and measures to theoretical constructs. Because Diaz-Guerrero and Holtzman used multiple operationalization in their study, it could be that there is a problem related to the way this illustration was set up and it is not a problem in the actual study. More checking is needed on this matter.

It has been demonstrated that there was a significant difference in the general knowledge test scores for those who viewed Plaza Sesamo and those who did not.[19] After consideration of the rival explanations in the internal validity and statistical conclusion validity categories, there appears to be no highly plausible rival explanation for the observed impact. Consideration of the explanations in the external validity and construct validity categories suggests that there are problems in generalizing the observed results to other times, settings, and persons or across treatments and measures to theoretical constructs.

Summary and Conclusions

There are, of course, several different experimental evaluation research designs that utilize randomization for the assignment of cases to treatment and control groups. The one discussed here is the classical experimental design known as the pretest-posttest control group design. Experimental designs are the most powerful evaluation research designs because they provide unequivocal control over most rival explanations in the internal validity category. Thus these designs make possible the strongest causal inferences. It is a general rule that experimental designs should be utilized whenever feasible.

The fact that experimental evaluation research studies are feasible is clear because approximately 150 social action program experiments have been conducted in the past few years.[20] The most prominent use of experimental designs in the development field appears to have been in the area of family planning. Individuals interested in reading about the details of these experiments in the development field should begin by consulting the overview provided by Elizabeth T. Hilton and Arthur A. Lumsdaine.[21] The general feasibility of conducting randomized experiments in field settings has been assessed by Cook and Campbell. They concluded their analysis by being "guardedly optimistic" about the prospects for such studies.[22] Furthermore, they identified nine types of "major obstacles to conducting true experiments in field settings"[23] and ten "situations conducive to field experiments."[24] Their analysis would seem to be of general relevance for the development field and readers interested in a detailed discussion of these topics are encouraged to consult their work.

Unfortunately, randomized experiments are not without problems. As in the case of preexperimental and quasi-experimental designs, there are potential applied research problems concerning the formulation of meaningful impact hypotheses, measurement concerns, and organizational resistances, and there are potential research utilization problems concerning factors such as the timing and relevance of studies. There also may be special ethical and cost problems when a randomized field experiment is conducted. I will turn to a detailed consideration of these potential problems in the next two chapters and I will assess the relative strengths and weaknesses of the various evaluation research designs in light of them.

NOTES

1. Rogelio Diaz-Guerrero and Wayne H. Holtzman, "Learning by Televised 'Plaza Sesamo' in Mexico," *Journal of Educational Psychology* 66 (1974): 632.
2. Ibid.: 632.
3. Ibid.: 633.
4. Ibid.: 633-634.
5. Ibid.: 633.
6. Ibid.: 632-643.
7. Ibid.: 633.
8. The data and report on the analysis can be found in ibid.: 637.
9. Ibid.: 633.
10. Ibid.: 634.
11. Thomas D. Cook and Donald T. Campbell, "The design and conduct of quasi-experiments and true experiments in field settings," in M. D. Dunnette, ed., *Handbook of Industrial and Organizational Research* (Chicago: Rand McNally, 1976): 229.
12. Diaz-Guerrero and Holtzman, "Learning by televised 'Plaza Sesamo' in Mexico": 634.
13. Ibid.: 633, 637.
14. Ibid.: 637.

15. Ibid.: 637.

16. Ibid.: 632-643.

17. Ibid.: 636-639.

18. Ibid.: 632-643.

19. Interestingly these same researchers and some associates found that this result did not hold in a later yet somewhat different experimental study of the impact of Plaza Sesamo. Cf., Rogelio Diaz-Guerrero, Isabel Reyes-Lagunes, Donald B. Witzke, and Wayne H. Holtzman, "Plaza Sesamo in Mexico: an evaluation," *Journal of Communication* 26 (1976): 155-164.

20. Robert F. Boruch, "Bibliography: illustrative randomized field experiments for planning and evaluation," mimeo, Evanston, Illinois, Northwestern University, 1974.

21. Elizabeth T. Hilton and Arthur A. Lumsdaine, "Field trial designs in gauging the impact of fertility planning programs," in Carl A. Bennett and Arthur A. Lumsdaine, eds., *Evaluation and Experiment: Some Critical Issues in Assessing Social Programs* (New York: Academic Press, 1975): 319-408.

22. Cook and Campbell, "The design and conduct of quasi-experiments and true experiments in field settings": 318.

23. Ibid.: 299-309.

24. Ibid.: 309-318.

Chapter 5

APPLIED RESEARCH PROBLEMS

The most serious limitations to the use of evaluation research concern applied research problems, those problems that arise in the actual use of the evaluation research methodology. These problems will vary in importance from study to study, but they are potentially widespread and serious enough to raise questions regarding the feasibility of using the evaluation research methodology to study the impact of a wide variety of development activities.

Impact Hypotheses

A requirement of evaluation research is that there are meaningful impact hypotheses regarding some aspect of a social action program. In some studies the impact hypotheses will be dictated by theory and therefore will be meaningful from a theoretical standpoint. This probably will occur most frequently in scholarly studies, but it will also happen when the social action program strategies are derived from an axiomatic theory. There are definite advantages in deriving impact hypotheses from a formal theory, but given the current state of development theory, it is unlikely that many meaningful hypotheses will be arrived at in this manner in the near future. In most instances the development impact hypotheses will be of an ad hoc nature, although consistent with a paradigmatic orientation, and will be based on the circumstances surrounding a specific activity. However, even a meaningful ad hoc impact hypothesis will not be possible for many development activities.

One reason is that development activities frequently are not of a size and nature to make it reasonable to expect them to have a measurable impact. For example, many technical assistance efforts involve a single advisor who works on a short-term project that results in a feasibility report or some other document that will not have a direct manifest impact.[1] Other technical assistance enterprises involve fellowships and manpower training projects with only very indirect impacts.[2] Numerous technical assistance projects involve pilot studies with no intended direct impact. For many development activities a systematic evaluation research study would not be worth the effort because of the size and nature of the activity.

Even if these problems are not present, it still may be difficult to identify impact variables. It is commonly suggested in the evaluation research literature that one start with the project or program goals and proceed to develop a set of impact variables which represent goals and possible side effects. However, problems of identifying goals of development activities are complex.[3] Many development activities have no apparent goals, some have goals that are stated ambiguously, and others have multiple and often conflicting goals where the relative importance is not clear. Other development activities have objectives that are not stated in easily measurable terms because legislators and bureaucrats rarely think in those terms. Furthermore, most development activities take place in an unstable setting. This often results in changing program goals. In addition, decisions on development activities are the result of a political process where domestic and international politics may be overwhelmingly important and lead to activities where a common set of goals has not been considered. In many cases great difficulty will be encountered in identifying meaningful impact variables that represent the range of possible impacts of development activities.

There are also problems in identifying independent variables for impact hypotheses. There are undoubtedly various parts of any project or program that deserve systematic examination. Evaluation research studies have focused on a variety of program factors, such as the total program (e.g., the Plaza Sesamo experiment[4]), different levels of the program treatment (e.g., the New Jersey negative income tax experiment[5]), different strategies for implementing the program (e.g., the Taiwan family planning program[6]), or frequently a combination of program factors such as these. However, it should be anticipated that there will be difficulty in specifying which aspects of development activities are to be evaluated. Evaluation research in the development field is further complicated by the fact that projects are frequently not implemented as planned and changes are made often during the process of implementation. Special attention must be devoted to specifying the treatment to be evaluated.

There is an additional problem with the independent variable which may be of special salience for some technical assistance policy-makers: How can the impact of a particular agency's activities be evaluated when a program is conducted jointly with other agencies? In these circumstances the activity of the agency must be isolated and an experimental or quasi-experimental design should be set up within the general program evaluation research design so that the separate impact can be assessed. If this is not feasible, then the identification of the separate impact may not be possible. One observer has noted the difficulty of assessing accurately the separate impact of technical assistance activities:

> [I]t is clear that the impact of technical assistance on economic development in any one country at any one time is marginal and intertwined with a host of other factors, some of which will weigh far more heavily in the economic scales. For this reason, it is not possible to evaluate technical assistance to any country by comparing the acceleration of economic development (rise in per capita income, say) with changes in the scale or composition of the technical assistance programmes.[7]

Even if it is possible to specify the independent variable and the dependent variable in the impact hypothesis, it is still necessary to specify the relationship between the variables. Is the impact immediate or delayed? Is the relationship linear or curvilinear? Is it of a threshold nature? Are other variables of relevance and must they be controlled explicitly?[8] Furthermore, the range of the possible impact should be specified. How much movement in the impact variable can be expected? The problems in arriving at a specification of the relationship between variables in an evaluation research study in the development field may be difficult, but must be overcome for the full benefit of the inquiry to be realized.

It will not be easy to identify and to state clearly the impact hypotheses in the development field. I would venture a guess that a large majority of the current development activities in the world would not lend themselves to the specification of a meaningful impact hypothesis. This does not mean that the evaluation research approach cannot be used to examine development activities. It does mean that its utility is limited to situations where meaningful impact hypotheses can be specified. It would appear that it can make a valuable contribution in those cases.

It does not seem unreasonable to ask why there are so many development activities with no goals, ambiguous goals, conflicting goals, unclear strategies, nonsystematic implementation, and confusion regarding the anticipated impact. Given the highly political nature of the policy-making processes that produce most development activities, it would be naive to expect all development activities to be planned clearly. On the other hand, it would appear that a better job can be done of clarifying many of these matters even within a muddling-through policy-making process. By forcing clarification of the program and a statement in operational terms of the objectives of activities, evaluation research will expose many weaknesses of development activities. If this leads to a correction of the weaknesses and a clarification of troublesome ambiguities, then evaluation research will make a major contribution to the development field.

Measurement Concerns

Many studies in the development field have focused on data per se and not on data as an indicator or measure of some construct (the WHO smallpox eradication program case study in Chapter 2 is an example). There are problems with this approach, especially when the nonconceptual orientation is a reflection of the orientation of the development project being studied. A nonconceptual orientation for a development activity tends to focus the activity on a specific data goal and not on a more general objective.[9] Furthermore, a nonconceptual orientation for an evaluation research study makes it difficult to generalize the observed results to other areas, times, and settings. It would appear to be beneficial to create a body of theoretical knowledge that can be used in the development field for the design of social action programs and the planning of evaluation research studies. This cannot be done without working with constructs. The measurement rules, of course, provide the crucial link between the theoretical constructs and data.

However, even when a theoretical orientation is used, it is difficult to measure adequately the properties of many development constructs and there is little agreement on how to do so. In reading the development literature one is struck by how frequently constructs, such as development and modernization, are used without their exact meaning being clarified. It is, of course, problematical to attempt to measure a concept without ever defining it clearly. In many development studies there is no attempt at direct measurement of a construct, and an indicator is used. We are, however, still left with the problem of determining how adequate is the indicator, and little can be concluded if the original construct has not been clarified. It is recommended that the constructs be defined clearly and that multiple operationalization be considered.

The measurement problems are among the most serious potential problems for evaluation research studies in the development field.[10] They are, however, not just a problem for researchers in this field, although development specialists may be faced with a special set of problems. In the conclusion for a twenty-four scholar assessment of four large research projects in the field of quantitative international politics it was noted by Dina A. Zinnes and myself that "the most serious methodological problems lie in the area of measurement."[11] Researchers in the development field, as well as other scholars, need to become more aware of measurement concerns and to do a careful job of handling them. This effort will be aided by attention to construct validity concerns.

Data Collection Procedures

It is, of course, difficult to evaluate the utility of any data collection techniques or data sources without reference to the specific uses that are to be made of the data. Data problems are not peculiar to evaluation research, although they may be highlighted by it. It appears that in the foreseeable future special emphasis will need to be placed on making data collection a part of development activities. Researchers are encouraged to use multiple data sources and multiple data collection methods for multiple indicators. Every effort should be made to employ unobtrusive measures.[12]

As noted earlier, a store of documentary and statistical material is produced routinely and is available for evaluation research purposes. These secondary data are often aggregated and are available most frequently for geographical areas where a governmental unit has been in existence and has collected the data. In the development field such data may be found in official statistical sources (e.g., *Statistical Yearbook* of the United Nations[13]), data archives (e.g., Inter-University Consortium for Political Research at the University of Michigan), and published social science data collections (e.g., *World Handbook of Political and Social Indicators*[14]). Unfortunately, many of these data are of questionable reliability. There is also a great deal of missing data, definitions change, data collection processes change, data in many developing countries are available for only short periods, and definitions of terms like Gross National Product may vary with the governmental unit. Many of the available data, furthermore, do not lend themselves to answering interesting development questions.

Field research involves direct contact with the environment under study and an effort is made to collect original data through the use of a combination of observational and interviewing techniques, and an analysis of records. In general, field research data collection will be more useful for project evaluations where the unit of analysis is the individual than for program evaluations which focus on a highly aggregated unit of analysis, such as a nation-state. Although the details of the application of field research data collection techniques may be somewhat unique in the development field, the advantages and problems in their utilization are basically the same as in other fields.

If data problems are approached in creative ways, then meaningful data can be generated for the systematic evaluation of many development activities.[15] Special attention should be devoted to determining exactly what treatment was actually given by a development activity.

Data Analysis Techniques

The data analytic and statistical techniques to be used will vary according to the evaluation research design and data.[16] While there may not be optimal statistical solutions for all problems, it appears that reasonable solutions can be found for most of them. The data analysis problems in the development context are not in general different from those in other contexts. Because of the high level of expertise needed, it is recommended that researchers obtain expert statistical advice. Experts should be consulted at the beginning of an evaluation research effort so that the full range of statistical alternatives can be considered during the planning period for the study. Data analysis can be improved by careful attention to statistical conclusion concerns.

Ethical Concerns

There are potential ethical problems revolving around issues such as: (1) withholding treatment from control group cases; (2) confidentiality of information; (3) honesty in reporting evaluation results; and (4) termination of treatment without disruption of subjects' lives.[17] Ethical problems are probably most acute when a randomized field experiment is undertaken, but could effect any evaluation research study. There are numerous techniques for protecting privacy and staging innovations which can alleviate ethical problems. In the final analysis, if the potential ethical problems cannot be resolved, the planned evaluation should not be implemented. I agree with Henry W. Riecken and his associates when they comment: "We suggest that before policymakers and researchers undertake an experimental program they should satisfy themselves that the program will, with high probability, provide benefits that will outweigh any foreseeable adverse side effects or any loss of initiative or freedom of program participants."[18] It will probably be a rare case in the development field when ethical concerns will be of a sufficient magnitude to force the cancellation of the evaluation of a program or project.

Organizational Factors

If the evaluation research methodology is to be useful in assisting policy-makers in the development field, there is a need to overcome several organizational resistances to undertaking an evaluation research study. The most serious potential organizational problem lies with the resistance of bureaucracies to systematic evaluation and its implied change. At the heart of this resistance is the identification of the bureaucrats and agency with the program. This means that the evaluation becomes an assessment of the bureaucrats and agency, a very threatening project. As Donald T. Campbell notes: "If the political and administrative system has committed itself in advance to the correctness and efficacy of its reforms, it cannot tolerate learning of failure."[19] He suggests two remedies which have relevance for development agencies: (1) evaluation research should not be used in ad hominem research; and (2) "advocates . . . [should] justify new programs on the basis of the seriousness of the program rather than the certainty of any one answer and combine this with an emphasis on the need to go on to other attempts at solution should the first one fail."[20] The evaluation research methodology frequently cannot be used without the cooperation of the bureaucracy in regard to holding the design constant, identifying and articulating goals of development activities, determining relative importance of multiple objectives, collecting relevant data for analysis, and assisting in multiple replications of evaluation research studies.

Another potential organizational problem lies with the high level of research skill required for performing evaluation research. Obviously, evaluation research requires skills not commonly found in practitioners in the development field. There is a long and unresolved controversy regarding inside and outside evaluators and development agencies probably will want to resolve this controversy within their own traditions. At a minimum, some degree of in-house expertise will probably be required, if for no other reason than to monitor contracts with outside evaluators; and outside evaluators will probably be required for clearly specified and very technical subtasks. Each development agency will need to work out the correct balance for itself. [21] It would seem to be of considerable importance that someone with a high level of evaluation research skill be involved in planning the evaluation research study as the development activity is planned. In that way stronger designs will be used more frequently.

There are numerous potential organizational problems which can develop in the relationship between evaluators, whether inside or outside, and the program personnel. Personality, role, value, frame of reference, and institutional differences can lead to friction over data collection, record keeping, selection of program participants, and the timing and ability to hold constant the evaluation design. Among the suggestions for lessening these tensions are: (1) support from administrators; (2) involvement of practitioners in the evaluation; and (3) clear role definition and authority structure.[22]

The cost of evaluation research can be high and this fact can present a budget problem in a development agency. Most of the expenses of evaluation research studies will be related to data collection, and they will vary according to the study. All development activities do not require evaluation and all activities being evaluated do not require the same level of funding. Based upon the experience in evaluating domestic programs in the United States, it is suggested that between 1 and 2 percent of the total budget for development activities be allocated for systematic evaluation.[23] This percentage can be adjusted as experience is gained. Because of economies of scale it would seem advisable to begin by evaluating large development projects and programs.

Development activities frequently take place in an unstable and highly political setting. This will result in changing programs and priorities and in problems in implementing and evaluating development activities. Factors such as high turn-over of office-holders and bureaucrats, domestic conflict and strife, an inflationary economy, uncertain funding for the budget, changes in the international economic order, famines, and unemployment may mean that development planning is not meaningful, that development activities are not implemented as planned, that changes are made as the activity is implemented, or that the activity never occurs. Furthermore, many development activities involve substantial changes in the traditional way of life and result in resistances by the population to both the program and its implementation. In many developing countries there is such incomplete information regarding the state of affairs and the need for programs that development activities that are based on one set of assumptions may need to be changed as more information becomes available. Nonavailability of foreign experts, resentment against foreigners and foreign assistance, and cultural difficulties may result in problems in the implementation and evaluation of technical assistance activities. Resistance to control groups on the part of certain segments of the society may present serious problems in the evaluation of any development activity. In short, there are numerous factors in the task environment of an organization that may result in evaluation research difficulties.

In some instances the organizational problems will be so severe as to preclude the meaningful use of the evaluation research approach. A significant amount has been written regarding the problems in using evaluation research for the examination of social action programs in the United States.[24] If anything, the setting in which development activities occur seems more complex and on the surface it would appear that the organizational problems are even more pronounced in the development environment. A definitive discussion of these problems will need to wait until evaluation research has been used more widely in the development field. It is my feeling that many, but not all, potential organizational problems can be solved in an adequate manner through a flexible and creative effort on the part of the policy-makers and the evaluation researchers.

Evaluation Research Designs

The numerous impact hypotheses, measurement, data collection, data analysis, ethical, and organizational problems mean that many development activities cannot be examined in a meaningful manner through the use of the evaluation research methodology. I will venture the estimate that at least four-fifths of contemporary development activities cannot be examined meaningfully through the use of evaluation research because of applied research problems. Furthermore, applied research problems affect which evaluation research designs can be used in the studies that can be conducted. Although the design to be used in a specific study depends on the particular circumstances surrounding that study, it is, nevertheless, possible to make a few general statements about the situations where the various designs might be most useful in the development field.

Pretest-posttest control group design. This classical experimental design requires considerable control over the implementation of a development activity, including the ability to assign randomly the cases to experimental and control groups.[25] Because the randomized experiment is so closely controlled, it is potentially helpful on measurement, data collection, and data analysis issues. However, ethical problems can be acute with this design, it will usually be the most expensive of the designs, and the required methodological expertise is frequently higher than for other designs. Furthermore, there may be bureaucratic problems in holding constant the design and negative reactions from the task environment when this design is used. Nevertheless, in many instances the limited availability of the treatment or the timing of the activity will facilitate the use of a randomized experiment. Because it yields the most unambiguous causal inferences, it is the preferred design when it is feasible. The argument that the process of random assignment equates the experimental and control groups, and therefore controls certain rival explanations, is most convincing when the number of cases is large. Thus, this design is probably most plausible when the focus is on the individual as the unit of analysis. Other focuses, such as classroom, village, hospital, neighborhood, group, or plot of land, may also be examined meaningfully in a given situation. This design will probably be more helpful for evaluating projects than programs, and difficulty should be anticipated when the impact hypothesis deals with a highly aggregated unit such as nation-state or large city and the development activity has broad-aims regarding those units. When this design is utilized, it is strongly recommended that experts in experimental design be consulted during the planning stage and that special attention be paid to external validity concerns in order that the design yields information that can be generalized to other times, settings and units of analysis.

Interrupted time-series design with a nonequivalent no-treatment control group time-series. This design requires that data be available at equally spaced intervals for a reasonable period before and after the beginning of a development activity for a group that received the treatment and one that did not.[26] This probably means that the data were collected for some purpose other than the evaluation of the activity, are available in secondary sources, were compiled by a governmental entity that had been in existence for some time, and that the data are aggregated, although data on individuals may be available in some fields, such as education and health. It is likely that the time interval will be the year, although some data may also be available at monthly, weekly, daily, or hourly intervals. This design will probably be most useful in evaluating impact hypotheses involving entities that have remained stable over time, such as villages, cities, states, and for broadly aimed programs designed to have an impact that can be captured with aggregate data indicators, such as Gross National Product, percentage unemployed, crude live birth rate, agricultural production, and literacy rate. The use of this design will be limited because systematic time-series data for many variables are not available in many developing countries. The time-series data that are available may not be reliable, changes in definitions and reliability may occur over time, differences in data collection systems for various governmental units may preclude the use of meaningful nonequivalent control group cases, and this design may have more data analytic problems than the other designs. The potential ethical problems, required methodological expertise, and the cost should not be as great as with the experimental design, but because of the long time period there may be some difficulty in holding the design constant, and inputs from the political environment may present problems when this design is utilized. The biggest problem in its use is finding control group cases without the development activity which also meet data requirements. This design is strongest when used in a homogeneous setting where the data collection system and history are identical for treatment and control group cases. In that circumstance a strong control of rival explanations is possible. However, the design is also worth using in other situations. This is the strongest of the quasi-experimental designs and should be used whenever feasible if a randomized experimental design cannot be employed.

Interrupted time-series design. This design is quite similar to the last one in regard to the problems and limitations in its use.[27] It will be most helpful for evaluating broadly aimed programs through the use of aggregated secondary data. It has disadvantages in regard to the relative degree of flexibility on measurement issues and because of limitations of available time-series data in developing countries it may be constrained in regard to utility. There may also be data analysis problems. It is roughly comparable to the previous design in regard to cost, ability to hold constant the design, and required expertise. It will probably be used more frequently in the development field than the interrupted time-series design with a nonequivalent, no-treatment control group time-series because it does not require the location of meaningful nonequivalent control group cases. However, in many circumstances it is less convincing than the latter design in regard to causal inferences.

Untreated control group design with pretest and posttest. This design has the greatest potential for use in the development field of the quasi-experimental designs discussed here.[28] It does not require the random assignment of cases, as does the pretest-posttest control group design, or the long series of data at equally spaced intervals required by the interrupted time-series with a nonequivalent, no-treatment control group time-series and the interrupted time-series design. It can be used for evaluating broadly aimed programs through the use of aggregated secondary data and for evaluating projects that focus on selected individuals. It has advantages in regard to flexibility on measurement issues, data sources, data collection procedures (aggregate, observational, and interviewing data are of potential relevance), data reliability, changes in definitions and data reliability that occur over time, ability to hold the design constant, cost, and expertise. The biggest difficulty is finding meaningful nonequivalent control group cases. Furthermore, data analysis and ethical problems could be factors in any individual study.[29] This design is in general well worth undertaking when it is not possible to use a fully randomized experimental design or an extended time-series of data. It is potentially most useful when a homogeneous setting allows one to have some confidence that history, maturation, instrumentation, and testing effects are similar in both groups, and thus controlled, and when a large number of cases for each group can be obtained. This design is, however, the least convincing of the discussed quasi-experimental designs in regard to possible causal inferences, and in some circumstances it may even be misleading, as in the Indonesian rice program case study in Chapter 3.

Posttest-only design with nonequivalent groups. In the event an experimental or quasi-experimental design cannot be employed, evaluation researchers in the development field may want to use this inexpensive design[30] or an elaboration of it (e.g., cross-sectional correlational and regression designs, causal modeling[31]). This design and its variations make possible tests of covariation, even if frequently they are weak in regard to possible causal inferences, because of the failure to control rival explanations in a meaningful manner. In many development situations a well done rigorous and systematic correlational study will be better than no evaluation study or an impressionistic one. Peter H. Rossi suggests that correlational studies be used in a preliminary way to identify covariation and that experimental and quasi-experimental designs be used in follow-up studies to examine effectiveness.[32] The logic of such a position lies in the fact that correlation is a necessary but not sufficient condition for covariation.

One group pretest-posttest design. In many circumstances a study using this design will be better than no evaluation. This design may be useful especially for smaller projects, addressing questions where the answer is generally accepted but where a double check is needed, or examining relatively unimportant questions where some information would be helpful but where a full-scale experimental or quasi-experimental study does not seem justified. This design assures that cause and effect are temporally correct and presents correlational evidence.[33] It is quite weak in regard to controlling rival explanations and meaningful causal inferences are problematical when it is used.

One group posttest-only design. This design may also be useful for smaller projects. It appears to be employed frequently in the technical assistance field as experts are called upon to make one-shot evaluation visits to ongoing projects. This type of evaluation may present helpful insights but provides little meaningful causal information. The one group posttest-only design is the design of last resort.[34]

Consideration should also be given to the use of designs not specifically discussed here. In many circumstances it may be possible to employ a patched-up design that combines features of some of the experimental and quasi-experimental designs that have been discussed. Furthermore, Donald T. Campbell, Julian C. Stanley, and Thomas D. Cook have presented several other experimental and quasi-experimental designs that are slightly different from the ones discussed.[35] Any one of them may be relevant to a specific study. The evaluation research design for any development activity should be established in light of the circumstances surrounding that activity and consideration should be given to establishing designs within designs. Researchers must be creative and flexible in putting together experimental and quasi-experimental designs to rule out rival explanations in specific circumstances, employing the full range of controls available for all four types of challenges to the validity of the obtained empirical results.

The Uniqueness of Applied Research Problems in the Development Field

The types of applied research problems that will be encountered in the development field are no different from those found in developed countries. This should not surprise anyone. Why should science and its categories of potential applied research problems be culture bound? What is different in the developed and developing contexts is the nature and severity of the various applied research problems. In general, it appears that the applied research problems are more severe in the development context, although I would emphasize that the seriousness of applied research problems varies greatly according to situations.

There appear to be no inherent differences between the developing and developed contexts regarding the potential severity of ethical or data analysis problems, or in the researcher's ability to generate theoretically interesting impact hypotheses. To the extent that measurement concerns are conceptual ones, there should be no basic differences in measurement problems in the developing and developed contexts. However, the data problems will be considerably more serious in the development context. The developing countries generally collect considerably less and lower-quality data, and most of them have collected data for a shorter time than developed countries. Furthermore, there are probably more problems in doing field research in developing countries. These latter problems cover the full range from linguistic diversity and lack of widespread literacy to bureaucratic harrassment and governmental refusal to allow the researcher to conduct field research. The seriousness of the data problems in most developing countries means that there will be more serious problems in the development context in using the more powerful quasi-experimental research designs because they require that time-series data and/or nonequivalent control group data be available. Furthermore, applied research problems, such as generation of policy-relevant impact hypotheses, organizational resistances, and employment of randomization to assign cases to treatment and control groups, are potentially more serious in developing countries.

Any applied research problem that requires extensive and widespread cooperation or assistance from bureaucrats and scholars in the development field will probably be severe because cooperation and assistance normally require sympathy with and receptivity for the study. In general, this sympathy and receptivity for evaluation research studies will not exist as frequently in developing countries as in the United States.[36] In the U.S. context the legitimacy of the evaluation research approach is accepted by many individuals, although there is still considerable skepticism. Many scholars and governmental practitioners in America who deal with domestic concerns have been trained in the behavioral science tradition and are prepared to accept as legitimate and even valuable the use of scientific approaches such as evaluation research. Furthermore, there is a tradition in America of publicly challenging and debating the worth of governmental activities. These conditions do not exist in many developing countries. Numerous officials in developing countries will not tolerate studies which evaluate activities of their government and they have the power to forbid such exercises. In addition, many important individuals in developing countries, both scholars and policy-makers, have been educated in a tradition that results in their being skeptical if not outright hostile toward the behavioral science approach, of which evaluation research is a part. People educated in the Marxist and neo-Marxist traditions, and they comprise a large group, may be hostile to the evaluation research enterprise. Many individuals trained in nonquantitative traditions in disciplines such as law, history, sociology, and public administration, both in the United States and abroad, will be at least skeptical. Probably, there are even differences in receptivity to evaluation research among American domestic and development specialists. I would estimate that a larger percentage of American development specialists, both scholars and policy-makers, have been trained in a nonquantitative tradition and will not accord legitimacy to evaluation research. What all of this means is that the receptivity to evaluation research studies will be generally lower in the development context than it has been in the American domestic context.

Does this mean that the applied research problems preclude the utilization of the evaluation research approach in the development context? I would say the answer is no. In many situations the applied research problem can be overcome and successful evaluation research studies can be conducted.

Becoming an evaluation researcher in the development field today is going to be quite a bit like becoming a downhill skier. There are certain basics to be learned, but actually doing the activity involves the application of the basics to constantly changing and often unique situations, where frequent, immediate, and successful problem solving is necessary for completion of the activity. In the beginning there may be many mistakes because the activity cannot be programmed in advance for every contingency and adjustments may be made too slowly. However, as the activity is repeated again and again and the terrain becomes familiar, the performance can be expected to improve and hints might even be given on how to do things successfully. Perhaps those that have done evaluation research in a developed country and begin doing evaluation research studies in the development context will find the experience a bit like those who have done cross-country skiing and then take up downhill skiing. Much of the jargon and many of the basics will be the same, but there is also much that is not the same and many things will need to be done differently.

Summary and Conclusions

All empirical research involves a series of methodological dilemmas, forcing on researchers decisions involving trade-offs. In order to control for a certain undesirable effect, it is often necessary to tolerate another hopefully more desirable but still less than satisfactory effect. If the research techniques that are used do not offer optimal solutions to all problems, they should, nevertheless, on balance be adequate. If properly used the evaluation research methodology has the potential for providing reliable impact evidence for use in the development field. However, while it is apparent that the evaluation research methodology is scientific, it is apparent also that overcoming applied research problems and using the evaluation research methodology in meaningful ways in the development field will be an art.

NOTES

1. William R. Leonard, Beat Alexander Jenny, and Offia Nwali report the following in regard to the 1967 technical assistance projects of the United Nations Development Program: (1) 66 percent of the projects involved single experts; (2) 16 percent of the projects involved two experts; and (3) 18 percent of the projects involved three or more experts. Cf., William R. Leonard, Beat Alexander Jenny, and Offia Nwali, *UN Development Aid: Criteria and Methods of Evaluation* (New York: Arno Press, 1971): 28-34.

2. During 1975 the World Health Organization spent approximately 8 percent of its regular budget on health manpower development. Cf., World Health Organization, *Financial Report 1 January — 31 December 1975,* Official Records of the World Health Organization, No. 230 (Geneva: World Health Organization, 1976): 35.

3. For insightful discussions of the problems in identifying program activities for evaluation research, see Edward A. Suchman, *Evaluative Research: Principles and Practice in Public Service and Social Action Programs* (New York: Russell Sage, 1967): 37-45; Joseph S. Wholey, John W. Scanlon, Hugh G. Duffy, James S.

Fukumoto, and Leona M. Vogt, *Federal Evaluation Policy: Analyzing the Effects of Public Programs* (Washington, D.C.: Urban Institute, 1973): 28-34; Carol H. Weiss, *Evaluation Research: Methods of Assessing Effectiveness* (Englewood Cliffs, N.J.: Prentice-Hall, 1972): 25-34; Joseph S. Wholey, Joe N. Nay, John W. Scanlon, and Richard E. Schmidt, "If you don't care where you get to, then it doesn't matter which way you go," in Gene M. Lyons, ed., *Social Research and Public Policies: The Dartmouth/OECD Conference* (Hanover, N.H.: University Press of New England, 1975): 181-185; and Peter H. Rossi, "Testing for success and failure in social action," in Peter H. Rossi and Walter Williams, eds., *Evaluating Social Programs: Theory, Practice and Politics* (New York: Seminar Press, 1972): 16-23. For a discussion of this topic in regard to development projects, see Samuel P. Hayes, Jr., *Evaluating Development Projects* (Paris: United Nations Educational, Scientific and Cultural Organization, 1966): 20-30.

4. Rogelio Diaz-Guerrero and Wayne H. Holtzman, "Learning by televised 'Plaza Sesamo' in Mexico," *Journal of Educational Psychology* 66 (1974): 632-643.

5. Cf., David N. Kershaw, "The New Jersey negative income tax experiment: a summary of the design, operations and results of the first large-scale social science experiment," in Lyons, ed., *Social Research and Public Policies:* 87-116.

6. Ronald Freedman and John Y. Takeshita, *Family Planning in Taiwan: An Experiment in Social Change* (Princeton, N.J.: Princeton University Press, 1966): 109-147.

7. Benjamin Higgins, "The evaluation of technical assistance," *International Journal* 25 (1969-1970): 37. Leonard, Jenny, and Nwali agree: "Any sorting out, particularly of benefits, with the objective of showing what part of them resulted from United Nations assistance, would have to employ very arbitrary methods and assumptions." See Leonard, Jenny, and Nwali, *UN Development Aid:* 17.

8. For a discussion of intervening variables, see Weiss, *Evaluation Research:* 47-53.

9. For a discussion of this point see Donald T. Campbell, "Assessing the impact of planned social change," in Lyons, ed., *Social Research and Public Policies:* 35-39.

10. For discussions of measurement problems in the evaluation research field, see Weiss, *Evaluation Research:* 34-53; Suchman, *Evaluative Research:* 115-131; Henry Riecken, Robert F. Boruch, Donald T. Campbell, Nathan Caplan, Thomas K. Glennan, Jr., John W. Pratt, Albert Rees, and Walter Williams, *Social Experimentation: A Method for Planning Social Intervention* (New York: Academic Press, 1974): 117-151; Jum C. Nunnally and William H. Wilson, "Method and theory for developing measures in evaluation research," in Elmer L. Struening and Marcia Guttentag, *Handbook of Evaluation Research,* Volume 1 (Beverly Hills: Sage Publications, 1975): 227-288; and Jum C. Nunnally and Robert L. Durham, "Validity, reliability, and special problems of measurement in evaluation research," in Struening and Guttentag, eds., *Handbook of Evaluation Research:* 289-352.

11. Francis W. Hoole and Dina A. Zinnes, "Summary, conclusions and implications," in Francis W. Hoole and Dina A. Zinnes, eds., *Quantitative International Politics: An Appraisal* (New York: Praeger, 1976): 468.

12. Cf., Eugene J. Webb, Donald T. Campbell, Richard D. Schwartz, and Lee Sechrest, *Unobtrusive Measures: Nonreactive Research in the Social Sciences* (Chicago: Rand McNally, 1966); and Thomas D. Cook and Donald T. Campbell, "The design and conduct of quasi-experiments and true experiments in field settings," in M. D. Dunnette, ed., *Handbook of Industrial and Organizational Research* (Chicago: Rand McNally, 1976): 319-321.

13. United Nations, *Statistical Yearbook* (New York: United Nations, annually since 1948).

14. Bruce M. Russett, Hayward R. Alker, Jr., Karl W. Deutsch, and Harold Lasswell, *World Handbook of Political and Social Indicators* (New Haven, Conn.: Yale University Press, 1964).

15. For discussions in the evaluation research literature of data collection procedures and problems, see Carol H. Weiss, "Interviewing in evaluation research," in Struening and Guttentag, eds., *Handbook of Evaluation Research:* 355-395; Abbott S. Weinstein, "Evaluation through medical records and related information systems," in Struening and Guttentag, eds., *Handbook of Evaluation Research:* 397-481; and Weiss, *Evaluation Research:* 53-59. For a discussion of these topics in the development field, see Hayes, *Evaluating Development Projects:* 31-80.

16. For an overview of relevant data analysis techniques, see Cook and Campbell, "The design and conduct of quasi-experiments and true experiments in field settings": 247-318; Donald T. Campbell and Julian C. Stanley, *Experimental and Quasi-Experimental Designs for Research* (Chicago: Rand McNally, 1963); Riecken et al., *Social Experimentation:* 73-116; Herbert W. Eber, "Multivariate methodologies for evaluation research," in Struening and Guttentag, eds., *Handbook of Evaluation Research:* 553-570; Donald T. Campbell and Albert Erlebacher, "How regression artifacts can mistakenly make compensatory education look harmful," in J. Hellmuth, ed., *Compensatory Education: A National Debate,* Volume 3 (New York: Brunner/Mazel, 1970): 185-210; William L. Hays, *Statistics for Psychologists* (New York: Holt, Rinehart and Winston, 1963); J. Johnston, *Econometric Methods* (Tokyo: McGraw-Hill Kogakusha, 1972); Glen G. Cain and Harold W. Watts, "Problems in making policy inferences from the Coleman Report," in Rossi and Williams, eds., *Evaluating Social Programs:* 73-95; and James S. Coleman, "Reply to Cain and Watts," in Rossi and Williams, eds., *Evaluating Social Programs:* 97-107.

17. For excellent general discussions of the potential ethical problems involved in evaluation research, see Riecken et al., *Social Experimentation:* 245-269; and Gideon Sjoberg, "Politics, ethics and evaluation research," in Marcia Guttentag and Elmer L. Struening, eds., *Handbook of Evaluation Research,* Volume 2 (Beverly Hills: Sage Publications, 1975): 29-51.

18. Riecken et al., *Social Experimentation:* 247.

19. Donald T. Campbell, "Reforms as experiments," *American Psychologist* 24 (1969): 410.

20. Campbell, "Assessing the impact of planned social change": 35.

21. For general staffing recommendations, see Wholey et al., *Federal Evaluation Policy:* 82-85, 117-118.

22. Weiss, *Evaluation Research:* 104-107.

23. For additional information on the US experience, see Wholey et al., *Federal Evaluation Policy:* 77-82; and Ilene N. Bernstein and Howard E. Freeman, *Academic and Entrepreneurial Research: The Consequences of Diversity in Federal Evaluation Studies* (New York: Russell Sage, 1975): 140.

24. For an examination of the organizational problems and suggestions for handling them, see Riecken et al., *Social Experimentation:* 153-243; Weiss, *Evaluation Research:* 92-109; Suchman, *Evaluative Research:* 132-168; Wholey et al., *Federal Evaluation Policy:* 28-85; Noralou P. Roos, "Evaluation, quasi-experimentation, and public policy," in James A. Caporaso and Leslie L. Roos, Jr., eds., *Quasi-Experimental Approaches: Testing Theory and Evaluating Policy* (Evanston, Ill.:

Northwestern University Press, 1973): 281-304; Kershaw, "The New Jersey negative income tax experiment": 87-116; Peter Rossi, "Field experiments in social programs: problems and prospects," in Lyons, ed., *Social Research and Public Policies:* 117-130; Henry W. Riecken, "Memorandum on program evaluation," in Carol H. Weiss, ed., *Evaluating Action Programs: Readings in Social Action and Education* (Boston: Allyn and Bacon, 1972): 98-104; David K. Cohen, "Politics and research: evaluation of social action programs in education," in Weiss, ed., *Evaluating Action Programs:* 137-165; Peter H. Rossi, "Boobytraps and pitfalls in the evaluation of social action programs," in Weiss, ed., *Evaluating Action Programs:* 224-235; Robert S. Weiss and Martin Rein, "The evaluation of broad-aim programs: difficulties in experimental design and an alternative," in Weiss, ed., *Evaluating Action Programs:* 236-249; Egon G. Guba, "The failure of educational evaluation," in Weiss, ed., *Evaluating Action Programs:* 250-266; Sidney H. Aronson and Clarence C. Sherwood, "Researcher versus practitioner: problems in social action research," in Weiss, ed., *Evaluating Action Programs:* 283-293; Carol H. Weiss, "Evaluation research in the political context," in Struening and Guttentag, eds., *Handbook of Evaluation Research:* 13-26; David Twain, "Developing and implementing a research strategy," in Guttentag and Struening, eds., *Handbook of Evaluation Research:* 27-52; Lee Gurel, "The human side of evaluating human services programs: problems and prospects," in Guttentag and Struening, eds., *Handbook of Evaluation Research:* 11-28; Rossi, "Testing for success and failure in social action": 11-49; Glen G. Cain and Robinson G. Hollister, "The methodology of evaluating social action programs," in Rossi and Williams, eds., *Evaluating Social Programs:* 109-137; Peter H. Rossi, "Observations on the organization of social research," in Rossi and Williams, eds., *Evaluating Social Programs:* 267-286; Walter Williams, "The capacity of social science organizations to perform large-scale evaluative research," in Rossi and Williams, eds., *Evaluating Social Programs:* 287-314; Chris Argyris, "Creating effective research relationships in organizations," in Francis G. Caro, ed., *Readings in Evaluation Research* (New York: Russell Sage, 1971): 100-112; and Hyman Rodman and Ralph Kolodny, "Organizational strains in the researcher-practitioner relationship," in Caro, ed., *Readings in Evaluation Research:* 117-136.

25. For elaboration on the pretest-posttest control group design and the advantages and limitations of its use, see Campbell and Stanley, *Experimental and Quasi-Experimental Designs for Research:* 13-34; Robert S. Weiss and Martin Rein, "The evaluation of broad-aim programs: experimental design, its difficulties, and an alternative," *Administrative Science Quarterly* 15 (1970): 97-109; John Oliver Wilson, "Social experimentation and public-policy analysis," *Public Policy* 22 (1974): 15-37; Alice M. Rivlin, "Allocating resources for policy research," *American Economic Review* 64 (1974): 346-354; Robert F. Boruch and Henry W. Riecken, "Final report: application of randomized experiments to planning and evaluating AID Programs," mimeo, Washington, D.C., Agency for International Development, October, 1974; Cook and Campbell, "The design and conduct of quasi-experiments and true experiments in field settings": 298-318; and Riecken et al., *Social Experimentation:* 1-85.

26. For elaboration on the interrupted time-series design with a nonequivalent no-treatment control group time-series, see Campbell and Stanley, *Experimental and Quasi-Experimental Designs for Research:* 55-57; Riecken et al., *Social Experimentation:* 97-105; Campbell, "Assessing the impact of planned social change": 15-23; Cook and Campbell, "The design and conduct of quasi-experiments and true experiments in field settings": 277-279; Donald T. Campbell and H. Laurence Ross, "The

Connecticut crackdown on speeding: time series data in quasi-experimental analysis," *Law and Society Review* 3 (1968): 43-46; Campbell, "Reforms as experiments": 417-419; and H. Laurence Ross, Donald T. Campbell, and Gene V. Glass, "Determining the social effects of a large reform: the British 'Breathalyser' crackdown of 1967," *American Behavioral Scientist* 13 (1970): 493-509.

27. For elaboration on the interrupted time-series design, see Campbell and Stanley, *Experimental and Quasi-Experimental Designs for Research:* 37-43; Riecken et al., *Social Experimentation:* 105-108; Campbell, "Assessing the impact of planned social change": 15-23; Cook and Campbell, "The design and conduct of quasi-experiments and true experiments in field settings": 274-277; Campbell and Ross, "The Connecticut crackdown on speeding": 41-43; Campbell, "Reforms as experiments": 412-417; and, Ross, Campbell, and Glass, "Determining the social effects": 494-496.

28. For elaboration on the untreated control group design with pretest and posttest, see Campbell and Stanley, *Experimental and Quasi-Experimental Designs for Research:* 47-50; Riecken et al., *Social Experimentation:* 108-113; and Cook and Campbell, "The design and conduct of quasi-experiments and true experiments in field settings": 249-256.

29. On the data analysis problems regarding this design, see Campbell and Erlebacher, "How regression artifacts": 185-210; and Thomas D. Cook and Charles S. Reichardt, "Guidelines: statistical analysis of nonequivalent control group designs: a guide to some current literature," *Evaluation* 3 (1976): 136-138.

30. For elaboration on the posttest-only design with nonequivalent groups, see Cook and Campbell, "The design and conduct of quasi-experiments and true experiments in field settings": 249; Riecken et al., *Social Experimentation:* 115-116; and Campbell and Stanley, *Experimental and Quasi-Experimental Designs for Research:* 8, 12-13.

31. Cf., Cook and Campbell, "The design and conduct of quasi-experiments and true experiments in field settings": 284-298; and Campbell and Stanley, *Experimental and Quasi-Experimental Designs for Research:* 64-71.

32. Rossi, "Boobytraps and pitfalls": 235; Rossi, "Testing for success and failure": 47-48; and Peter H. Rossi, "Evaluating social action programs," in Caro, ed., *Readings in Evaluation Research:* 279-281.

33. For elaboration on the one group pretest-posttest design, see Cook and Campbell, "The design and conduct of quasi-experiments and true experiments in field settings": 247-248; Riecken et al., *Social Experimentation:* 113-114; Campbell and Stanley, *Experimental and Quasi-Experimental Designs for Research:* 7-12; and Campbell and Ross, "The Connecticut crackdown on speeding": 37-41.

34. For elaboration on the one group posttest-only design, see Cook and Campbell, "The design and conduct of quasi-experiments and true experiments in field settings": 247; and Campbell and Stanley, *Experimental and Quasi-Experimental Designs for Research:* 6-7.

35. Cf., Campbell and Stanley, *Experimental and Quasi-Experimental Designs for Research:* 24-34, 43-47, 50-55, 57-64; and Cook and Campbell, "The design and conduct of quasi-experiments and true experiments in field settings": 256-274, 279-284.

36. For an excellent discussion of the general problem in another substantive context, see Richard R. Fagen, "Studying Latin American politics: some implications of a *Dependencia* approach," *Latin American Research Review* 12 (1977): 3-26.

Chapter 6

RESEARCH UTILIZATION PROBLEMS

Sophisticated and potentially useful decision-making aids such as evaluation research are limited in impact unless policy-makers utilize the results from them. It is, therefore, of importance to ask how and where evaluation research fits into the policy-making process and what the major problems are likely to be in employing it as an aid for policy-makers in the development field.

A Muddling-Through Policy-Making Process

Any meaningful examination of research utilization problems must begin with a consideration of the policy-making process. A policy-making process consists of the series of events involved in making and executing decisions. If evaluation research is to influence policy-making, it must do so by providing information that is used in the policy-making process. Thus, research utilization problems can be seen as problems involved with the use of evaluation research information in the policy-making process. From a policy-making perspective, evaluation research is concerned with the provision of systematic feedback on organizational impacts and the possible influence of evaluation research information is constrained by the feedback possibilities of any particular policy-making process.

All policy-making processes in the public sector have certain things in common. Each is essentially a political process where a number of policy-makers engage in a struggle over proposed actions. Most policy-making processes are structured and complex, and can usefully be viewed as cybernetic systems. Inputs consist of information that comes into a policy-making process and is transformed by it. Outputs are the system's products, which are called actions. The system is the mechanism that transforms inputs into outputs. Feedback consists of information regarding results of actions which is fed back into the system as a subsequent input.

The focus here will be on the budgetary process in the World Health Organization (WHO). The purpose is to present a description of what appears on the surface to be a more or less typical policy-making process in the development field, so as to set the scene for a discussion of evaluation research utilization problems. More detailed information is available in my book entitled *Politics and Budgeting in the World Health Organization.* [1] Undoubtedly certain aspects of policy-making would be different for other agencies and for nonbudgetary policy-making processes, although the overall picture is fairly typical for the development field.

It is worth noting in passing that certain aspects of the WHO budgetary process are considered to be among the more creative in the development field and that participation in the WHO budgetary process is considered by many to be good training for policy-makers from developing countries. Furthermore, the WHO budgetary process has influenced the development of budgetary processes in the development context, especially in the health field. Certainly, the World Health Organization would have to be considered to be one of the most successful of the agencies working in the development field.

It is, of course, the participants in the WHO budgetary process who evaluate inputs and decide upon organizational budgetary actions.* There are seven major types of policy-

---

* Most of the material in this and the following nine paragraphs originally appeared in Francis W. Hoole, Brian L. Job, and Harvey J. Tucker, "Incremental budgeting and international organizations," *American Journal of Political Science* 20,2 (1976): 273-301. I am grateful to Wayne State University Press and my coauthors for permission to use the material here.

makers in WHO: (1) governmental diplomats, who are members of the parliamentary bodies of WHO and can be seen as playing the same general role as elected representatives (e.g., senators, city councilmen) in other policy-making processes; (2) governmental technical representatives, who are members of the parliamentary bodies of WHO and are also responsible for their country's portion of WHO development activities (they are both representatives and bureaucrats for the WHO member states); (3) the executive head (Director-General of WHO), who is elected by the parliamentary bodies to be in charge of the administrative operations of the agency and performs the same general role in the WHO budgetary process as prime ministers, presidents, governors, and mayors in other systems; (4) members of the secretariat, who are international civil servants and make up the bureaucracy of WHO; (5) representatives of other international governmental organizations, who may be viewed as being similar to diplomats from other countries in a nation-state system; (6) representatives of nongovernmental organizations, who may be viewed as being similar to interest group representatives in other systems; and (7) experts, who are selected because of their technical expertise and serve in their personal capacity.

The policy-makers take into account a variety of information when producing organizational actions. Inputs from sources within the institution that are based upon normal organizational factors are considered to be organizational inputs. Organizational history and precedents help form an incremental basis for policy-making while organizational goals, program repertoires, and availability of information all condition the responses of the institution to particular situations. Information originating from sources outside the organization is considered to be an external input. Examples include communications from other political institutions, demands from nongovernmental agencies in the task environment, and relevant new scientific and technological information. Inputs that are based upon special innovations rather than upon organizational or external factors are considered to be leadership inputs.

In interacting in a budgetary process, which is, of course, highly political, the policy-makers appear to develop patterns of behavior, which have been expressed by scholars as behavioral policy-making rules. A policy-making rule is the calculus by which information coming into a policy-making process is transformed into organizational action. Such a rule expresses outputs as specific functions of particular inputs and is a statement of the behavior of policy-makers on a specific issue. The politics of policy-making are contained in policy-making rules, which in the WHO budgetary process appear to be highly incremental and disjointed.

The cycle of events involved in the planning, approval, and execution of an annual budget for WHO extends over a period of nearly four years and involves five analytically distinct steps or subsystems. Each of these steps in the budgetary process occurs during a different period in time and each involves distinct organizational actions. Furthermore, each step involves a slightly altered situation with potential differences existing in inputs, activities of policy-makers, and policy-making rules. The division of the budgetary process into steps reflects the tendency in WHO, as in other organizations, to partition complex problems into manageable subproblems, which are then solved sequentially. An overview of the WHO budgetary process is presented in Figure 6.1.

The proposal development step involves preparation of specific proposals for action, which are presented in the Director-General's budget document. This step lasts eighteen months and ends approximately ten months before the start of the fiscal year in question. The activity associated with this step takes place primarily outside the parliamentary bodies of WHO and essentially involves the executive head, members of the secretariat, and governmental technical representatives. In their budget proposals the Directors-General of WHO have focused upon justification of the change in the budget from the one approved for the prior year by the World Health Assembly. This step can be viewed as being similar to the one in other budgetary processes where the president's, prime minister's, governor's, and mayor's budgets are prepared.

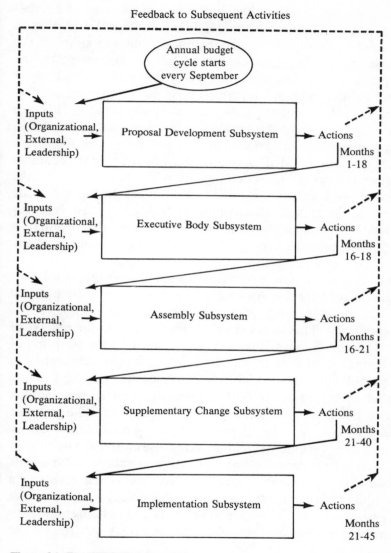

Figure 6.1: The WHO Budgetary Process

The executive body step involves review of the budget proposal by the Executive Board of WHO. The WHO Executive Board consists of approximately 20 percent of the members of the Assembly and exists to oversee administration of the agency, to make decisions in a limited area of competence, and to screen proposals going to the World Health Assembly. This step, which extends from the time of the release of the Director-General's budget document to the adoption of a resolution on the budget by the executive body at its annual February meeting, lasts approximately three months, during months sixteen to eighteen of the budget cycle. This step ends approximately ten months before the start of the fiscal year in question. The primary policy-makers are the executive head, governmental diplomats, and governmental technical representatives. Formal debate and informal negotiation take place in the Executive Board, and a budget proposal may be approved, amended, tabled or, conceivably, rejected. It seems reasonable to view the budgetary actions as the result of a bargaining process engaged in by the policy-makers at the Executive Board session.

The assembly step involves adoption of a budget resolution by the World Health Assembly. Each member state has one vote in the Assembly, which is the supreme WHO policy-making body. This step extends from the time of the release of the Director-General's budget document until the adoption of the budget resolution by the Assembly at its annual meeting in May and lasts approximately six months, during months sixteen to twenty-one of the budget cycle. It ends seven months before the start of the fiscal year in question. The primary policy-makers are the executive head, governmental diplomats, and governmental technical representatives. The assembly step is best described as legislative in nature and it seems reasonable to view the budgetary actions as the result of a bargaining process engaged in by the policy-makers at the assembly meeting. This step may be viewed as being similar to the one in other processes where the congress, parliament, or city council approves budgets.

Numerous changes may be made to the resolution after its adoption by the Assembly. These activities comprise the fourth step in the budgetary process, which is called the supplementary change step. Changes involve formal amendment of the approved resolution or adjustments within specific limits by the executive head. When the change requires a formal amendment to the resolution a proposal must be developed and the Executive Board or Assembly will usually consider it. This step begins immediately following the assembly step and is concluded at the end of the fiscal year in question. It lasts approximately twenty months, during months twenty-one to forty of the budget cycle. In WHO the supplementary changes have been for a variety of purposes ranging from buildings to special assistance for health crises in the member states. They appear to have been justified on the basis of special external and leadership factors, and not by appeal to organizational circumstances. It seems reasonable to view the budgetary actions at this step as the result of a bargaining situation which involves essentially the executive head, members of the secretariat, governmental technical representatives, and perhaps, governmental diplomats. This step may be viewed as being similar to the supplementary change step found at federal, state, and municipal levels in various countries and in the policy-making processes of other development agencies.

The fifth step in the budgetary process involves carrying out the approved budget resolution. This includes the hiring of staff, purchase of materials, and detailed execution of the program of action contained in the budget. This step, which is called the implementation step, often has the effect of changing the approved resolution through interpretation and implementation. Activity during this step involves primarily the members of the secretariat, governmental technical representatives, and the executive head. The implementation step in WHO is similar to the one found at the federal, state, and municipal levels in many countries and in the policy-making processes of other development agencies. It involves spending the money authorized in the budget. In WHO the implementation step begins immediately following the assembly step and is concluded five months after the end of the fiscal year in question. It lasts twenty-five months, during months twenty-one to forty-five of the budget cycle. The first eight months of this period, those between the end of the annual assembly meeting in May and the start of the fiscal year on the following

January 1, are concerned with establishing plans of operation, hiring staff, and ordering supplies. The next twelve months of this step, months twenty-nine to forty of the budget cycle, are those of the fiscal year in question, and the budget plans are executed. The last five months of the step are concerned with concluding the reporting on the implementation that took place during the fiscal year. A financial report, auditor's report, and an annual report on the activities of the organization during the year are produced. The step ends with their consideration at the annual Assembly meeting during May of the following calendar year.

Each of these steps should be viewed as a subsystem with its own inputs, outputs, feedback, and process characteristics. Each subsystem in the budget process has a different set of potential inputs because each step takes place at a different point in time. Division of the process into five subsystems means that there are five sets of relevant policy-making rules. One of the most striking features of the process is its complexity. Numerous policy-makers representing varieties of viewpoints are dealing simultaneously with numerous overlapping issues. Information is incomplete and rationality is bounded. The system is cybernetic, and bargaining and negotiation occur throughout it. The inputs are changing constantly and the general decision-making environment is fluid and above all else highly political. The policy-making process is not unlike that described by Aaron Wildavsky, John P. Crecine, and Graham T. Allison for other political situations.[2] The making and implementing of budgetary decisions in WHO is essentially a process where numerous policy-makers become involved at various policy-making steps in a struggle over institutional actions. Meta-concerns, such as the north-south and east-west conflicts, place constraints on the entire policy-making process.

The WHO development activities, by their nature, are joint efforts on the part of WHO and the host country's government. Frequently a development activity will be a joint product of several institutions, such as WHO, the host country's government, the government of another country, another international governmental organization, and a nongovernmental foundation. This means that the WHO development programs are the product of several autonomous policy-making systems and that the degree of complexity involved is potentially greater than when only a single institution such as a national development agency is engaged in an activity. In the case of WHO the between-system as well as the within-system problems must be resolved before a successful program can be undertaken.

The World Health Organization appears to be so overwhelmed by cross-cutting political currents and complicated task environments that the policy-makers reduce complexity and ambiguity, and are able to make decisions, by focusing on budgetary matters in modest incremental terms. The WHO budgetary process is a version of what Charles E. Lindblom has called a muddling-through policy-making process.[3]

What differences in the budgetary process are likely to be found in other development agencies? Obviously the timing of the process may be different; the beginning and the length of various steps in the budgetary process may vary in other annual budgetary cycles; and some agencies may be on biannual or even longer cycles. Furthermore, the budgetary steps may vary in other agencies, with the most likely differences being found at the executive body, assembly, and supplementary change steps. In some budgetary processes one or more of these steps may be unimportant or even nonexistent, while in other budgetary processes their relative importance may vary. There may also be differences in the types and relative importance of policy-makers, although I suspect that these differences will not be very significant. There may also be differences in the details of the policy-making rules, although I think that most policy-making rules in budgetary processes in the development field will be of an incremental nature. I personally feel that the WHO budgetary process is a muddling-through budgetary process which is in many ways typical in the development field and that the differences between it and most other development budgetary processes probably would be ones of degree.

What differences are likely to be found in nonbudgetary processes, both in WHO and in other development agencies? The differences in the steps in the policy-making process and the role of the policy-makers are likely to be primarily ones of degree as regards budgetary and nonbudgetary processes in most development agencies. Furthermore, the nature of the policy-making rules is not likely to differ greatly on budgetary and nonbudgetary matters, although the use of incrementalism may be more obvious and widespread on budgetary matters. However, the timing of the policy-making process may be quite different for budgetary and nonbudgetary concerns. The budgetary cycle proceeds in a relatively fixed manner with the relatively nonflexible schedule and the necessity for a budget resulting in the setting of deadlines which force actions to be taken at certain times. On nonbudgetary matters the timing and necessity for action will be more irregular and the policy-making process will not force frequently the taking of actions in quite the same way. The analysis of the potential research utilization problems in the WHO budgetary process should provide insights regarding potential research utilization problems in nonbudgetary processes and hopefully will provide the basis for comparative analyses on this topic in the development field.

Adding an Evaluation Research Subsystem

Using Alice M. Rivlin's perspective, evaluation research can tell what actually works.[4] Even though it may be known that a treatment works in perfect conditions, as do the high-yielding varieties of rice and as does smallpox vaccination, there is still the question of whether the social action program of an agency is being administered in such a manner that it is having the desired societal impact. The promise of evaluation research is that it can provide systematic information on the actual impact of organizational activities and feed this information back into the policy-making process in such a way that subsequent decisions can be made regarding those activities.

The WHO budgetary process, like most other development policy-making processes, is a cybernetic one with constant adjustments being made in activities as the organization adapts to circumstances in its environment.[5] The most meaningful way of minimizing evaluation research utilization problems is to integrate the evaluation research approach into the policy-making process, rendering it a decision-making aid which can be used as appropriate by policy-makers to provide timely feedback information on the impact of ongoing activities of interest to them. The most obvious way of integrating evaluation research into the WHO budgetary process would be to add a sixth budgetary step, called the evaluation research subsystem. An overview of such a hypothetical WHO budgetary process is presented in Figure 6.2.

The evaluation research subsystem would involve the planning and execution of specific impact studies of activities contained in the budget. Because it is preferable that evaluation research studies be designed as the organization's development activities are being planned, it is best to conceive of beginning the evaluation research subsystem during the first month of the budget cycle. Throughout the initial twenty-eight months of this cycle the evaluation research studies could be planned and pretest data could be collected. The activity implementation for a specific budget would take place during the appropriate fiscal year, which occurs during months twenty-nine to forty of the budgetary cycle. Depending on the evaluation research design and the frequency of data collection (e.g., daily, weekly, monthly, yearly) and analysis, there may or may not be relevant feedback information available during this period. The last five months of the evaluation research subsystem, months forty-one to forty-five of the annual budget cycle, could involve data collection, data analysis, and the preparation of reports. From time to time additional analyses would be completed during the following months. The output from this subsystem would be evaluation research findings.

The activities associated with this step would take place primarily outside the parliamentary bodies of WHO and would involve primarily the executive head, members of the secretariat, and governmental technical representatives. Experts in the methodology of evaluation research might also be involved

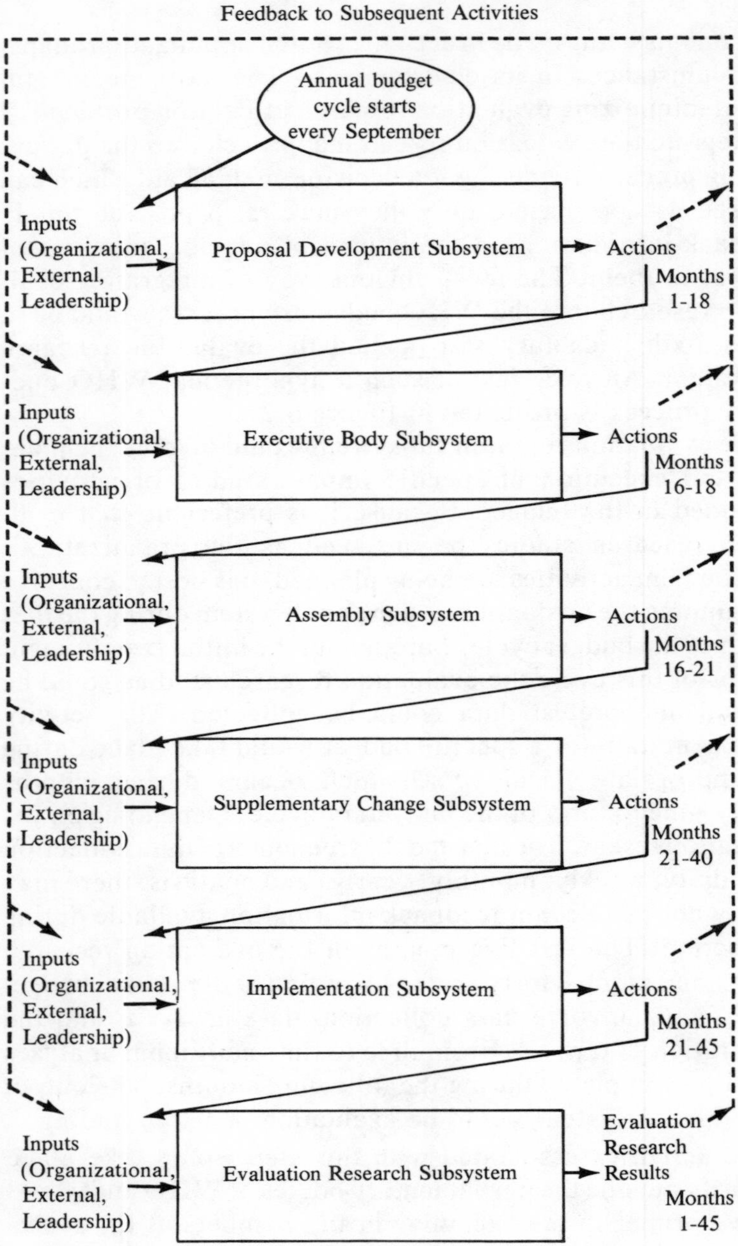

Feedback to Subsequent Activities

Figure 6.2: The WHO Budgetary Process after Addition of
          Evaluation Research Subsystem

as consultants. The evaluation research subsystem and its activities would be constrained by the full range of organizational, external, and leadership inputs. The political factors from the remainder of the budgetary process probably would manifest themselves in the evaluation research subsystem and affect the design, execution, and reporting of evaluation research studies.

As the evaluation research results were fed back into the WHO budgetary process, they would become inputs into subsequently occurring subsystems. The evaluation research results would be only a small part of the total information available. In fact, the WHO budgetary process is already overloaded with information. Furthermore, there is limited room for innovation, it is mainly on the margins, and other input factors are extremely important in the highly political budgetary process. Because the policy-makers have already established patterns of behavior, called policy-making rules, which transform inputs into actions, it is likely that the evaluation research results would be used frequently in a partisan manner to reinforce predispositions. It seems unlikely that there would be widespread or major changes in the policy-making rules because of evaluation research studies, at least in the beginning. The relevance of the knowledge contained in an evaluation research study would be a major factor in determining its utility.

The timing of the relatively fixed budget cycle would also have ramifications for how the evaluation research findings would be utilized. Because the budget cycle for a given year extends over a forty-five month period and because a new budget cycle begins each year, there is overlap in the activities for different fiscal years. This can be seen in Table 6.1, which assumes the addition of an evaluation research subsystem and provides information on the budgetary activities which would have occurred during the months of 1969. It can be seen which subsystems would have been in progress during a given month during 1969 and thus which subsystems for which fiscal years could have been effected by feedback during that month.

Table 6.1: WHO Budgetary Activities During 1969 Calendar Year

Month	Budgetary Activities for Various Fiscal Years					
	Evaluation Research Subsystem	Implementation Subsystem	Supplementary Change Subsystem	Assembly Subsystem	Executive Body Subsystem	Proposal Development Subsystem
January	1968, 1969, 1970, 1971	1968, 1969	1969	1970	1970	1970, 1971
February	1968, 1969, 1970, 1971	1968, 1969	1969	1970	1970	1970, 1971
March	1968, 1969, 1970, 1971	1968, 1969	1969	1970		1971
April	1968, 1969, 1970, 1971	1968, 1969	1969	1970		1971
May	1968, 1969, 1970, 1971	1968, 1969, 1970	1969, 1970	1970		1971
June	1969, 1970, 1971	1969, 1970	1969, 1970			1971
July	1969, 1970, 1971	1969, 1970	1969, 1970			1971
August	1969, 1970, 1971	1969, 1970	1969, 1970			1971
September	1969, 1970, 1971, 1972	1969, 1970	1969, 1970			1971, 1972
October	1969, 1970, 1971, 1972	1969, 1970	1969, 1970			1971, 1972
November	1969, 1970, 1971, 1972	1969, 1970	1969, 1970			1971, 1972
December	1969, 1970, 1971, 1972	1969, 1970	1969, 1970	1971	1971	1971, 1972

Let us assume that it was possible to complete an evaluation research study of certain 1968 budgeted activities and that the findings were presented in a report that was completed during May of 1969. To the extent that the findings had implications for the conduct of evaluation research studies they could have effected the ongoing evaluation of 1969 budgeted activities and the evaluation research studies planned for 1970 and later years. The findings could have effected the ongoing implementation of the 1969 budgeted activities and the implementation subsystem for following years. The same would have been true for the supplementary change subsystem. However, the evaluation research findings for the 1968 budgeted activities could have had their first real impact in the assembly, executive body, and proposal development subsystems for the 1971 budget year (it is not likely that the information would have been studied quickly by members of the assembly and used to affect the assembly decisions on the 1970 budget). With careful management of the timing of the evaluation research study a slight improvement possibly could have been made and earlier budget years could have been effected. However, the room for manipulation of the timing is quite limited.

How would evaluation research information be used in the WHO budgetary process? It seems unlikely that it would have a major annual impact in the executive body and assembly subsystems. The policy-making at these steps is conditioned by the budget from the preceding step and changes in it are rarely made. The most effective use of the evaluation research approach in these subsystems would probably not lie in its use to influence annual decisions but in its use over the long term to hold the executive head and members of the secretariat accountable by making them show that they have accomplished something, by making them justify financial support by establishing their legitimacy in general terms. It is somewhat more likely that evaluation research results would have an impact annually in the supplementary change subsystem. Minor changes could be made in ongoing activities during this step. It is most likely that evaluation research results would be useful in the implementation subsystem as activities are carried out and in the proposal development subsystem as future activities are planned. The effect in the implementation subsystem would be most likely for the two succeeding budget years while the effect in the proposal development subsystem would be most likely for the third and later budget years. The policy-makers associated most closely with these subsystems are the executive head, members of the secretariat, and governmental technical representatives. Thus they are the policy-makers that are most likely to use the evaluation research results on a regular basis for policy-making.

What are the ramifications of the timing of the budgetary process for the choice of evaluation research designs? There is a dilemma in regard to the use of designs employing time-series data. The strongest causal inferences from quasi-experimental designs are possible when time-series data are used, but designs using time-series data have serious research utilization problems because of the timing of the policy-making process. It is recommended that serious consideration be given to collecting time-series data at intervals more frequent than the year (e.g., day, week, month) and to anticipating future knowledge needs and setting up designs employing time-series data so that information can be produced before the launching of major new development activities. Because most posttest-only designs are limited in terms of causal inference they are not very useful. The most helpful designs would be the untreated control group design with pretest and posttest and the pretest-posttest control group design, with the latter being preferred because of its strengths in regard to causal inferences. However, even those designs involve delays in regard to their possible effect on the planning for future activities in the proposal development subsystem.

What can be concluded in regard to the potential impact on the policy-making activities of the addition of an evaluation research subsystem to a muddling through process? In the last chapter I estimated that applied research problems dictated that perhaps only 20 percent of the development activities were legitimate candidates for systematic evaluation research studies. In this chapter I have argued that the timing involved in the policy-making process and its political nature present serious additional problems. Does this mean that evaluation research is potentially not useful for policy-makers in the development field? I would say no. It is probably more accurate to describe the scope of its potential as limited. The relevance of the knowledge and the timing of the studies will present the most serious research utilization problems in a muddling-through policy-making process.

A Modeling-Through Policy-Making Process

The literature is filled with discussions of quantitative public policy analysis techniques and debates concerning their ability to improve the policy-making process.[6] Some proposals, especially those of the 1960s, emphasized the development of models of the entire policy-making process and there were calls for comprehensive processes like those found in the planning, programming, budgeting (PPB)[7] and management information systems. The zero-base budgeting proposals of the 1970s would also appear to imply a comprehensive system. Nevertheless, the use of quantitative public policy analysis techniques is not limited to comprehensive systems. These techniques also could be used in disjointed, incremental, decentralized systems. Whenever quantitative public policy analysis models are used we have some form of what I will call a modeling-through policy-making process.

Many individuals feel that there is a need today to move toward modeling-through systems. For example, Bertram M. Gross, when discussing management strategies for economic and social development, argued: *"Decisionmaking . . . is a process of sequential model-using. Decisionmaking need not be 'muddling through,' but must be 'modeling through.' "*[8] It is, of course, an important question how far public agencies will be able to move from a muddling-through to a modeling-through process. My purpose here is not to assess the extent to which such changes are possible, nor to discuss the problems associated with them, but to provide a perspective on where evaluation research would fit in a modeling-through system, to discuss the relationship between evaluation research and other selected quantitative public policy analysis techniques, and to analyze the research utilization problems likely to be encountered in such a system by the evaluation research approach.

Figure 6.3 has a view of what a modeling-through system might look like in WHO. It shows where six of the more frequently discussed types of quantitative public policy analysis techniques might fit into the revised WHO budgetary process. A brief discussion follows of each of these types of techniques and its potential relationship with the evaluation research approach.

Planning and forecasting. Numerous techniques are available for the development of plans and forecasts. They range from extrapolations of trends using techniques such as the Box-Jenkins autoregressive moving average (ARIMA) models, to expanding the detailed budget assumptions over future years, to examination of hypothetical future scenarios through the use of econometric and computer simulation models.[9] In PPB systems a five-year budget forecast is developed frequently, with the budget forecast for the first year being the one submitted by the executive head for approval by the legislative bodies. Some agencies utilize the multiyear macroplan with specific targets for achievement. Naomi Caiden and Aaron Wildavsky have presented an excellent overview of planning practices in the development field in their book entitled *Planning and Budgeting in Poor Countries,*[10] which should be consulted by anyone interested in this topic. In the WHO budgetary process the planning and forecasting activities would be carried out primarily by the executive head, members of the secretariat, and governmental technical representatives. The use of quantitative analysis techniques for the development of plans and forecasts would be most useful in the proposal development subsystem. To the extent that the evaluation research information is useful in the development of assumptions which form the basis for plans and forecasts, and to the extent that the timing of the evaluation research studies allows for meaningful feedback, the evaluation research infor-

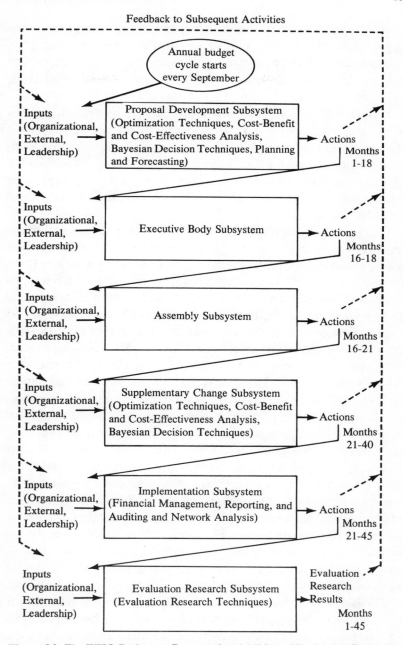

Figure 6.3: The WHO Budgetary Process after Addition of Evaluation Research
Subsystem and Selected Quantitative Public Policy Analysis Techniques

mation will be helpful in planning and forecasting efforts. It is likely that the evaluation research information would be filtered through cost-effectiveness, optimization, and bayesian decision techniques before being used in planning and forecasting.

Cost-benefit and cost-effectiveness. These techniques involve the evaluation of the ratio of cost to returns for an activity. They are part of a general approach to efficiency and are helpful especially when used comparatively for clarifying the potential consequences of alternative choices regarding the allocation of resources.[11] However, as Ronald W. Johnson and John W. Pierce note: "Cost-benefit analysis should be distinguished from cost-effectiveness analysis. Both costs and benefits are measured in terms of dollars in cost-benefit analysis whereas in cost-effectiveness analysis, benefits are not stated in dollar terms."[12] These techniques would appear to be most helpful in the proposal development subsystem of the WHO budgetary process, although they may also be used in the supplementary change subsystem to examine budgetary revisions. It is also possible that these techniques could be used at the implementation step for within-project and within-program analysis. Cost-benefit and cost-effectiveness studies could be given to the policy-makers at the executive body and assembly subsystems, but it is the executive head, members of the secretariat, and governmental technical representatives participating in the proposal development and supplementary change subsystems who would be most involved in the use of cost-benefit and cost-effectiveness techniques. Because evaluation research is addressed to the generation of reliable effectiveness information, the feedback from the evaluation research subsystem would be of most direct relevance for the cost-effective technique. The timing of the evaluation research study and its scope of knowledge will determine the meaningfulness of its effectiveness information.

Optimization techniques. There are various techniques, such as linear and nonlinear programming, that handle complex allocation of resources problems in such a manner as to provide an optimal mix of activities (e.g., project, program) that will best achieve an objective function, given a certain set of constraints.[13] These techniques would appear to be most helpful in the proposal development subsystem of the WHO budgetary process, although from time to time they might be used to examine possible budgetary revisions at the supplementary change step. It is also possible that these techniques could be used at the implementation step for within-project and within-program analysis. Optimization studies could be given to the policy-makers at the executive body and assembly subsystems, but it is the executive head, members of the secretariat, and governmental technical representatives participating in the proposal development and supplementary change subsystems who would be most involved in the use of optimization techniques. These techniques frequently require assumptions about how activities will work and how effective and efficient they will be, in short, assumptions about the social production function. To the extent that the evaluation research subsystem provides meaningful information that can be utilized in developing better assumptions, it will provide useful feedback for optimization techniques. The timing of the evaluation research study and its scope of knowledge again will determine its usefulness.

Bayesian decision techniques. Ward Edwards, Marcia Guttentag, and Kurt Snapper have recently suggested use of a decision-theoretic approach utilizing bayesian statistics and multiattribute utility analysis.[14] At the heart of the approach is the calculation of the probability of achieving certain end states such as goal attainment. The emphasis is on the calculation of subjective prior probabilities of items such as program success, which can then be recalculated as posterior probabilities after the information on program effectiveness is available. These techniques would appear to be most helpful in the proposal development subsystem of the WHO budgetary process, although from time to time they might be used to examine possible budgetary revisions in the supplementary change subsystem or, occasionally, changes within projects or programs in the implementation subsystem. It is likely that the executive head, members of the secretariat, and governmental technical representatives that are participating in the proposal development and supplementary change subsystems would be most directly involved in the use of these techniques. To the extent that the evaluation research subsystem provides information that can be used in the calculation of the posterior probabilities, it will provide useful feedback for bayesian decision techniques.

Network analysis. There is a group of modern management techniques which includes the program evaluation review technique (PERT) and critical path programming, and utilizes networking ideas. These techniques are concerned primarily with the scheduling and monitoring of the implementation of activities.[15] They emphasize managerial control of the implementation of activities and are potentially most useful in the implementation subsystem of the WHO budgetary process. It is most likely that network analysis would be used by the executive head, members of the secretariat, and governmental technical representatives. These techniques would be of benefit to the evaluation research subsystem to the extent that they lead to the careful implementation of activities, and they would be affected by evaluation research information to the extent that it leads to changes in the implementation of ongoing projects and the development of new networks.

Financial management, reporting, and auditing. There are numerous modern accounting and financial management systems which focus on the managing, reporting, and auditing of the financial aspects of activities. These systems are concerned with the proper dispersal of funds and are most useful in the implementation subsystem of the WHO budgetary process. It is likely that these analyses would be carried out by the executive head and members of the secretariat (and perhaps an outside auditor). It is doubtful that these systems and the evaluation research approach will frequently have a direct effect on one another.[16]

These various types of quantitative public policy analysis techniques are complementary, with each being addressed to a different yet not inconsistent matter. The information from them would appear to be most useful in the proposal development and implementation subsystems, with some limited utility in other subsystems. The discussed techniques probably are most helpful for the executive head, members of the secretariat, and governmental technical representatives. They would be constrained in their utility by the timing of the budgetary cycle and the fact that they would be used in a political process where factors other than long-range organizational concerns, efficiency, optimal mixes of activities, probability of success, scheduling of implementation, and sound financial management also would be of major significance. Budgetary processes appear to be dominated by bargaining and negotiation, and they tend to be disjointed and incremental in nature. It is likely that these techniques would be used to examine marginal changes and that they would be used in a partisan manner by policy-makers. The evaluation research approach would generate feedback information that would be most useful in cost-effectiveness, optimization, and bayesian decision analyses, although from time to time it might also effect planning and forecasting or network analyses. In general, the research utilization problems for the evaluation research approach in modeling-through systems, as in the case of muddling-through processes, will revolve around timing and relevance of information.

It is worth noting that cost-benefit and cost-effectiveness analysis, optimization techniques, network analysis, and financial management, reporting, and auditing focus primarily on the allocation and expenditure of resources. They would probably be of limited utility in a nonbudgetary policy-making process. The planning and forecasting approach, bayesian decision techniques, and evaluation research techniques are of potential utility in both budgetary and nonbudgetary policy-making processes. Each of the quantitative public policy analysis techniques attempts to help policy-makers understand a complex world, but does so by employing a complex methodology. The usefulness of these techniques obviously depends on the training and orientation of the policy-makers employing them. No policy-maker will decide an important matter on the basis of a methodology that is not understood and trusted. In this regard, the evaluation research methodology would seem to be the equal of the other techniques because the results from an evaluation research study can be plotted in diagrams, such as those presented in the earlier chapters of this book, and almost anyone can examine those diagrams and understand them.

Miscellaneous Caveats

The recent evaluation research literature contains assessments of research utilization problems that have been uncovered in the American domestic context. These discussions acknowledge that there are very serious research utilization problems for the evaluation research approach and frequently they offer suggestions for the solution of these problems. These discussions would appear to be of relevance in the development context. The more comprehensive and representative assessments will be presented here in an attempt to complement the previous discussion of research utilization problems.

Why are there research utilization problems? Joseph S. Wholey and his associates have noted that the "recent literature is unanimous in announcing the general failure to affect decision-making in a significant way."[17] They cited four basic reasons:

Organizational inertia. Organizations tend to resist change whereas evaluation usually implies change.

Methodological weakness. Policy-makers properly distrust the results of poorly done studies and rely instead on their own experiences or instincts.

Design irrelevance. Too many studies bear little or no relationship to the critical program and policy issues.

Lack of dissemination. The relevant decision-makers are not shown or briefed on the results of useful studies.[18]

Carol H. Weiss has noted that "A number of constraints frequently limit the use of evaluation results . . . : (1) the evaluator's perception of his role in the utilization process, (2) the organization's resistances to change, (3) inadequate dissemination of results, (4) the gap between evaluation findings and clear courses for future action, and (5) the tendency of much evaluation to show little or no positive effect."[19]

What should be done? Weiss argues that evaluation research studies must be made more relevant and suggests how this can be accomplished.

> Generally, it appears that for the evaluation to be relevant, agreement on several prior issues is essential: (1) the goals of the program, (2) the nature of program service (and any variants thereof), (3) measures that indicate the effectiveness of the program in meeting its goals, (4) methods of selection of participants and controls, (5) allocation of responsibilities for participant selection, data collection, descriptions of program input, etc., (6) procedures for resolving disagreements between program and evaluation personnel, and above all, (7) the decisional purposes that evaluation is expected to serve.[20]

Jeffery L. Pressman summarized the suggestions offered at a conference on evaluation research in the following terms:

(1) Evaluators should work more quickly.

(2) Government should be more interested in long-term problems.

(3) Both government officials and outside evaluators should try to identify policy problems before they become crises.

(4) Communication and personnel exchange between the user and evaluator communities should be increased.

(5) Users should create more incentives for doing high-quality evaluations.

(6) Universities should provide greater rewards for interdisciplinary and problem-oriented research.

(7) More attention should be paid to the presentation of evaluation research in clear and readable form.[21]

It seems to me that following the suggestions reported by Weiss and Pressman and using some common sense will alleviate some of the research utilization problems that are likely to arise in the development context.[22]

The Uniqueness of Research Utilization Problems in the Development Field

There are many similarities in the things that can be said about the uniqueness of research utilization problems in the development field and those things that were said in the last chapter about the uniqueness of applied research problems in the development field. The types of research utilization problems that will be encountered in the developing countries are no different than those found in developed countries. What is different is the nature and severity of the research utilization problems. In general, it appears that the research utilization problems are more severe in the development context.

Overcoming research utilization problems will require extensive efforts by policy-makers in developing countries, and it will not be an easy task because extensive efforts usually require a sympathy with and receptivity for what is being done. As discussed in the last chapter, there probably will not be a high level of sympathy and receptivity for evaluation research, and, in the near future, it will not be accorded the same legitimacy in most developing countries as it has received in the United States. However, it can be anticipated that there will be some sympathetic and responsive policy-makers in developing countries and when they are involved the research utilization problems will be overcome. The nature and severity of research utilization problems will vary from study to study and the solutions will depend on the cooperation of policy-makers involved in specific situations.

Are there different solutions for research utilization problems in developing and developed countries? The answer is no. In both contexts the use of an enterprising approach to research utilization problems which employs common sense, hard work, and the selective use of the advice offered in the caveats in the last section will be helpful. The old saying about being able to lead a horse to water but not being able to make it drink is appropriate here. It is possible to do much in specific circumstances about the timing and relevance of evaluation research studies. It is not possible to make individuals use the results from those studies, although it would appear likely that some certainly will if the results are relevant and timely. This circumstance is not unique to the development field.

Summary and Conclusions

Decisions on development activities are the result of political processes which tend to emphasize factors other than effectiveness evidence regarding ongoing activities. Evaluation research information will be used only if it is made meaningful for policy-makers. Organizations in the development field must work on (1) narrowing the gap between evaluation findings and action alternatives, (2) identifying meaningful ways of disseminating results, and (3) reducing delays in obtaining answers. These efforts can be facilitated by careful selection of evaluation research studies after a critical examination of political conditions, ethical considerations, methodological factors, and policy-making requirements.

There are likely to be severe research utilization problems as the evaluation research methodology is introduced into the development field. In the final analysis, no policy-maker wants to rely for an important decision on a policy-making technique that is not fully understood and trusted. When key decisions are made, most policy-makers will rely on the instincts and intuition that have served them throughout their lives. The most serious research utilization problem undoubtedly will be the resistance of policy-makers to changing their way of doing things. The key factor in research utilization problems will be the attitudes of policy-makers involved in the specific situations. There are no easy solutions for evaluation research utilization problems in the development context.

NOTES

1. Francis W. Hoole, *Politics and Budgeting in the World Health Organization* (Bloomington: Indiana University Press, 1976). This section also builds directly on Francis W. Hoole, Brian L. Job, and Harvey J. Tucker, "Incremental budgeting and international organizations," *American Journal of Political Science* 20 (1976): 273-304.

2. Cf., Aaron Wildavsky, *The Politics of the Budgetary Process* (Boston: Little, Brown, 1974); John P. Crecine, *Governmental Problem Solving: A Computer Simulation of Municipal Budgeting* (Chicago: Rand McNally, 1969); and Graham T. Allison, *Essence of Decision: Explaining the Cuban Missile Crisis* (Boston: Little Brown, 1971).

3. Charles E. Lindblom, "The science of muddling through," *Public Administration Review* 19 (1959): 79-88.

4. Cf., Alice M. Rivlin, *Systematic Thinking for Social Action* (Washington, D.C.: Brookings Institution, 1971): 86-119.

5. Karl W. Deutsch, *The Nerves of Government* (New York: Free Press, 1963); and John Steinbruner, *The Cybernetic Theory of Decision: New Dimensions of Political Analysis* (Princeton, New Jersey: Princeton University Press, 1974).

6. Cf., *A Study of the Capacity of the United Nations Development System,* Volumes 1 and 2 (Geneva: United Nations, 1969).

7. For an overview of PPBS, see Fremont J. Lyden and Ernest G. Miller, eds., *Planning, Programming, Budgeting: A Systems Approach to Management* (Chicago: Markham, 1972).

8. Bertram M. Gross, "Management strategy for economic and social development: part II," *Policy Sciences* 3 (1972): 14.

9. Cf., G.E.P. Box and G. M. Jenkins, *Time Series Analysis: Forecasting and Control* (San Francisco: Holden-Day, 1970); Charles R. Nelson, *Applied Time Series Analysis for Managerial Forecasting* (San Francisco: Holden Day, 1973); William G. Sullivan and W. Wayne Claycombe, *Fundamentals of Forecasting* (Reston, Virginia: Reston, 1977); Steven C. Wheelwright and Spyros Makridakis, *Forecasting Methods of Management* (New York: John Wiley, 1977); and Thomas H. Naylor, ed., *Computer Simulation Experiments with Models of Economic Systems* (New York: John Wiley, 1971).

10. Naomi Caiden and Aaron Wildavsky, *Planning and Budgeting in Poor Countries* (New York: John Wiley, 1974).

11. For an introduction to cost-benefit and cost-effectiveness analysis, see Jerome Rothenberg, "Cost-benefit analysis: a methodological exposition," in Marcia Guttentag and Elmer L. Struening, eds., *Handbook of Evaluation Research,* Volume 2 (Beverly Hills: Sage Publications, 1975): 55-88; Henry M. Levin, "Cost-effectiveness analysis in evaluation research," in Guttentag and Struening, eds., *Handbook of Evaluation Research:* 89-122; Ronald W. Johnson and John M. Pierce, "The economic evaluation of policy impacts: cost-benefit and cost-effectiveness analysis," in Frank P. Scioli, Jr., and Thomas J. Cook, eds., *Methodologies for Analyzing Public Policies* (Lexington, Mass.: Lexington Books, 1975): 131-154; William R. Leonard, Beat Alexander Jenny, and Offia Nwali, *UN Development Aid: Criteria and Methods of Evaluation* (New York: Arno Press, 1971): 95-103; and John H. Noble, Jr., "The limits of cost-benefit analysis as a guide to priority-setting in rehabilitation," *Evaluation Quarterly* 1 (1977): 347-380.

12. Johnson and Pierce, "The economic evaluation of policy impacts": 133.

13. For an introduction to optimization techniques, see Stuart S. Nagel with Marian Neef, *Operations Research Methods: As Applied to Political Science and the Legal Process* (Beverly Hills: Sage Publications, 1976); and R. Stansbury Stockton, *Introduction to Linear Programming* (Homewood, Ill.: Richard D. Irwin, 1971).

14. Ward Edwards, Marcia Guttentag, and Kurt Snapper, "A decision-theoretic approach to evaluation research," in Elmer L. Struening and Marcia Guttentag, eds., *Handbook of Evaluation Research,* Volume 1 (Beverly Hills: Sage Publications,

1975): 139-181. For introductory information on the bayesian approach, also see R. E. Peterson and K. K. Seo, "Public administration planning in developing countries: a bayesian decision theory approach," *Policy Sciences* 3 (1972): 371-378; Marcia Guttentag, "An approach to evaluation," unpublished paper SHC.75/WS/3, United Nations Educational, Scientific and Cultural Organization, Paris, 3 February, 1975; Marcia Guttentag, "Subjectivity and its use in evaluation research," *Evaluation* 1 (1973): 60-65; Marcia Guttentag, "Evaluation of social intervention programs," *Annals of the New York Academy of Sciences* 218 (1973): 3-13; Marcia Guttentag and Kurt Snapper, "Plans, evaluations, and decisions," *Evaluation* 2 (1974): 58-64, 73-74; and Ward Edwards and Marcia Guttentag, "Experiments and evaluations: a reexamination," in Carl A. Bennett and Arthur A. Lumsdaine, eds., *Evaluation and Experiment: Some Critical Issues in Assessing Social Programs* (New York: Academic Press, 1975): 409-463.

15. For an introduction to network analysis, see Leonard, Jenny, and Nwali, *UN Development Aid:* 69-95; and Daniel D. Roman, "The PERT system: an appraisal of program evaluation review technique," in Herbert C. Schulberg, Alan Sheldon, and Frank Baker, eds., *Program Evaluation in the Health Fields* (New York: Behavioral Publications, 1969): 243-253.

16. For an excellent presentation of the interface between traditional auditing concerns and evaluation research concerns, see *Effectiveness Auditing in Government Administration, Goals and Methods for Examining the Effectiveness of Central Government in Sweden, Summary of a Report of the Swedish National Audit Bureau 1970,* The Swedish National Audit Bureau.

17. Joseph S. Wholey, John W. Scanlon, Hugh G. Duffy, James S. Fukumoto, and Leona M. Vogt, *Federal Evaluation Policy: Analyzing the Effects of Public Programs* (Washington, D.C.: Urban Institute, 1973): 46.

18. Wholey et al., *Federal Evaluation Policy:* 50.

19. Carol H. Weiss, *Evaluation Research: Methods of Assessing Program Effectiveness* (Englewood Cliffs, N.J.: Prentice-Hall, 1972): 110.

20. Carol H. Weiss, "Between the cup and the lip . . . ," *Evaluation* 1 (1973): 54.

21. Jeffery L. Pressman, "Decisionmakers and evaluators: some differences in perspective and possible directions for the future," in Gene M. Lyons, ed., *Social Research and Public Policies: The Dartmouth/OECD Conference* (Hanover, N.H.: University Press of New England, 1975): 203-204.

22. For additional background on research utilization problems, see Joseph S. Wholey, Joe N. Nay, John W. Scanlon, and Richard E. Schmidt, "Evaluation: when is it really needed?" *Evaluation* 2 (1975): 89-93; Carol H. Weiss, "The politicization of evaluation research," *Journal of Social Issues* 26 (1970): 57-68; Nathan Caplan, "Factors associated with knowledge use among federal executives," *Policy Studies Journal* 4 (1976): 229-234; Carol H. Weiss, "Policy research in the university: practical aid or academic exercise?" *Policy Studies Journal* 4 (1976): 224-228; Janet A. Weiss, "Using social science for social policy," *Policy Studies Journal* 4 (1976): 234-238: Robert F. Boruch, "Problems in research utilization: use of social experiments, experimental results and auxiliary data in experiments," *Annals of the New York Academy of Sciences* 218 (1973): 56-77; Carol H. Weiss, "Where politics and evaluation research meet," *Evaluation* 1 (1973): 37-45; Carol H. Weiss, "The meaning of research utilization," paper prepared for the American Society for Public Administration Meetings, Washington, D.C., April 21, 1976; Carol H. Weiss, "Utilization of evaluation: toward comparative study," in Carol H. Weiss, ed., *Evaluating Action Programs: Readings in Social Action and Education* (Boston:

Allyn and Bacon, 1972): 318-326; Joseph S. Wholey, "What can we actually get from program evaluation?" *Policy Sciences* 3 (1972): 361-369; Herbert C. Schulberg and Frank Baker, "Program evaluation models and the implementation of research findings," in Schulberg, Sheldon, and Baker, eds., *Program Evaluation in the Health Field:* 562-572; Peter H. Rossi and Sonia R. Wright, "Evaluation research: an assessment of theory, practice, and politics," *Evaluation Quarterly* 1 (1977): 6-7; Edward A. Suchman, *Evaluative Research: Principles and Practice in Public Service and Social Action Programs* (New York: Russell Sage, 1967): 144; Victor G. Nielsen, "Input-output models and the nonuse of policy analysis," in Michael J. White, Michael Radnor, and David A. Tansik, eds., *Management and Policy Science in American Government* (Lexington, Mass.: Lexington Books, 1975): 195-203; Noralou P. Roos, "Evaluation, quasi-experimentation, and public policy," in James A. Caporaso and Leslie L. Roos, eds., *Quasi-Experimental Approaches: Testing Theory and Evaluating Policy* (Evanston, Ill.: Northwestern University Press, 1973): 281-304; Floyd Mann and Rensis Likert, "The need for research on the communication of research results," in Francis G. Caro, ed., *Readings in Evaluation Research* (New York: Russell Sage, 1971): 146-149; Nathan Caplan, "Social research and national policy: what gets used, by whom, for what purposes, and with what effects," in Marcia Guttentag with Shalom Saar, eds., *Evaluation Studies Review Annual,* Volume 2, 1977 (Beverly Hills: Sage Publications, 1977): 351-359; Laurence E. Lynn, Jr., "Policy relevant social research: what does it look like?" in Guttentag with Saar, eds., *Evaluation Studies Review Annual:* 63-76; Howard R. Davis and Susan E. Salasin, "Applied social research: in combat with waste and suffering," in Guttentag with Saar, eds., *Evaluation Studies Review Annual:* 320-326; Rehka Agarwala-Rogers, "Why is evaluation research not utilized?" in Guttentag with Saar, eds., *Evaluation Studies Review Annual:* 327-333; and Gary B. Cox, "Managerial style: implications for the utilization of program evaluation information," *Evaluation Quarterly* 1 (1977): 499-508.

Chapter 7

CONCLUSIONS, IMPLICATIONS, AND RESEARCH NEEDS

This chapter is both conclusion and commencement. It attempts to fit things into context by presenting conclusions, implications, and suggestions for research.

Conclusions

The best way to improve the quality of research on the impact of development activities is to improve the way in which questions are asked and answers are obtained. The major contribution of this book undoubtedly will be to make readers more sensitive to the evaluation research approach to answering these questions. Hopefully development specialists will then begin emphasizing a falsification strategy by focusing on both impact hypotheses and plausible rival hypotheses and begin using evaluation research designs which allow reliable causal inferences to be made. Clearly, the ideas of evaluation research can be of help in planning more adequate research strategies for tests of specific impact hypotheses regarding social action programs in the development context.

Evaluation research, as does any research approach, has its limitations, and it is not a panacea that will eliminate the difficulty inherent in evaluating the impact of development activities. These activities involve complex tasks which are attempted in difficult environments. Evaluating their impact is always problematical. The primary advantage of the evaluation research approach is that more dependable cause and effect statements are possible. There are also side benefits. Evaluation research forces clarification of what the treatment or program consists of and necessitates a statement in operational terms of the objectives of the activities. It has the potential for providing valuable impact information, provided that it is used in a sensible manner with its limitations as well as its advantages being understood. Development scholars and policy-makers should give serious consideration to learning more about evaluation research and its use.

Evaluation research may be of assistance to scholars in setting up research designs when cause and effect statements of the impact of development activities are being examined. It may be of special interest to those development scholars who are seeking to give policy relevance to their work because it leads frequently to a bridging of the gap between academic and policy concerns.

The most serious difficulties for scholars in utilizing evaluation research are of an applied research nature. There is a shortage of relevant and reliable data in many developing countries. There is little agreement on how to measure many concepts. Evaluation research is relatively expensive. Ethical problems may arise concerning issues such as withholding treatment from control groups, confidentiality of information, and termination of treatment without disruption of subjects' lives. Furthermore, the level of methodological expertise needed to handle many research problems is high. The seriousness of these and other problems will vary from study to study and they are not unique to the development context, although their exact nature and severity may be unique. Development scholars will need to do the best they can in any given circumstances, handling problems in a flexible and creative manner.

The potential uses and advantages for the policy-maker are generally the same as for the scholar. The potential problems for the policy-maker are more numerous. The same difficulties in applying the methodology exist for both the scholar and policy-maker. Several additional problems, such as relevance of knowledge and timing of studies, must also be overcome if evaluation research is to be helpful to policy-makers.

The difficulties are not sufficient to preclude the use of the evaluation research approach by development policy-makers. Carol H. Weiss has noted that: "The [evaluation] research process takes more time and costs more money than offhand evaluations that rely on intuition, opinion, or trained sensibility, but it provides a rigor that is particularly important when (1) the outcomes to be evaluated are complex, hard to observe, made up of many elements reacting in diverse ways; (2) the decisions that will follow are important and expensive; and (3) evidence is needed to convince other people about the validity of the conclusions."[1] These conditions frequently confront policy-makers in the development field. They should use the evaluation research approach when this happens. Evaluation research could be especially helpful to policy-makers in demonstrating their organization's accomplishments to those to whom they are responsible, especially those who are paying for the activities.

However, the history of evaluation research in the United States suggests that it would be a mistake to expect too much in the development field from evaluation research, just as it would be a mistake to dismiss it as having nothing to offer. Evaluation research techniques are helpful in certain circumstances in assisting policy-makers in handling the complexity of their environment. The evaluation research techniques, therefore, should be introduced carefully into the arsenal of decision-making aids available to policy-makers in the development field, and they should be used when needed for meaningful analysis.

Implications

Suggestions concerning the education of present and future development scholars and policy-makers are implicit in this discussion. Clearly, the educational emphasis on substantive development problems must be continued. However, it should be supplemented with education in evaluation research. There is a need to develop standard semester-long courses on the topic of evaluation research and development activities for students in undergraduate and graduate schools. Likewise, short courses and summer institutes on this topic should be established for mid-career individuals. Making development scholars and policy-makers better informed regarding evaluation research by means of the educational process should help promote the meaningful use of the evaluation research methodology in the development context.

A central clearinghouse on the topic of evaluation research and development activities is needed. Such a clearinghouse could facilitate communication among policy-makers and scholars using evaluation research to examine development activities by promoting newsletters, organizing meetings, providing a depository for evaluation research studies and data in the development field, conducting literature searches, maintaining an up-to-date multilingual bibliography, and facilitating the carrying out of other similar activities as appropriate. Perhaps a section of a professional society should be organized around the topic of evaluation research and development activities. These ideas could be facilitated by the establishment of the clearinghouse infrastructure at an institution such as the United Nations Institute for Training and Research. Perhaps the personnel associated with the clearinghouse could perform some of the educational functions mentioned earlier.

There are implications for the funding decisions of organizations in the development field. Agencies should be willing to fund meaningful evaluation research studies of their development activities and to provide released time for the evaluation research education of civil servants. Grants providing time for scholars to learn about and use evaluation research in the development context are also in order. There is little likelihood that there will be significant use of evaluation research in the development field without adequate financial support to get things started.

Finally, because good theory gives meaning and guidance for evaluation research studies, emphasis should be placed on the use of theory in evaluation research studies in the development field. When an impact hypothesis is derived from a theory, there is an explanation for the hypothesis. Furthermore, when the hypothesis is falsified, there is frequently a basis for revising the theory and deriving a new hypothesis which can serve as the basis for modifications in development activities and new scholarly studies. The use of theory can give meaning and order to various studies and assist in the systematic development of cumulative knowledge. Unfortunately, the current state of theory in the development field will make the immediate use of theory a difficult task. The point is that theory building should become a major goal in the development field and immediate emphasis should be placed on starting work on meaningful development theories.

Research Needs

This book obviously does not present the final word regarding evaluation research and development activities. It makes only a modest beginning in the clarification of the study of the impact of development activities and the utility of evaluation research. Considerable work remains to be done and hopefully the material presented here will be helpful in that task.

In addition to using evaluation research to study substantive questions, researchers should begin to document systematically the problems of using evaluation research in the development field. A significant amount has been written regarding the problems in using evaluation research for the examination of the impact of social action programs in the United States. A contribution could be made by clarification of problems in the development context. Not only do we need to know which impact hypotheses are tenable, we also need to know more about when it is possible to use evaluation research in the development field. The excellent analyses by Donald T. Campbell, Howard E. Freeman, Henry W. Riecken, Alice M. Rivlin, Peter H. Rossi, Edward A. Suchman, Carol H. Weiss, and Joseph S. Wholey have raised a number of interesting points; what is needed is consolidation, refinement and systematic extension into the development field of this work.

Evaluation researchers must avoid falling into the same trap that they are urging others to avoid. Evaluation researchers have been arguing that it should not be assumed that social action programs are actually having impacts on the social system, and they have argued that the evaluation research methodology should be utilized to determine exactly what kind of impact is being made. Yet they have been assuming that evaluation research will have an impact on the quality of scholarly research and on the policy-making process. Even if we accept that the evaluation research methodology has an impact in highly controlled circumstances, as do smallpox eradication and green revolution techniques, we need to ask whether it will have an impact on complex policy-making processes and scholarly disciplines. If evaluation research should be used to assess the actual impact of social action programs, then it should be used to assess the actual impact of the evaluation research methodology. I, therefore, suggest that the following impact hypothesis and variations of it be tested: the use of the evaluation research methodology results in an improvement in the quality of development activities and scholarly research. It can be anticipated that it will be difficult to set up appropriate experimental and quasi-experimental designs that will rule out alternative explanations and provide adequate examinations of the causality involved in such a hypothesis. However, if evaluation researchers believe that their approach is relevant and that it is the best way to obtain impact information, then they should be willing to test this hypothesis and variations of it, employing their own methodology to evaluate the impact of their own methodology.

A Final Perspective

I have tried to avoid the excesses of cheers or condemnation for evaluation research. The fact is that the evaluation research methodology is neither as useful as many of its proponents suggest, nor as useless as many of its opponents suggest. I am optimistic that it can be used meaningfully in the development context.

NOTE

1. Carol H. Weiss, *Evaluation Research: Methods of Assessing Program Effectiveness* (Englewood Cliffs, N.J.: Prentice-Hall, 1972): 2.

BIBLIOGRAPHY

Abt, C. C., ed., *The Evaluation of Social Programs* (Beverly Hills: Sage, 1977).

Agarwala-Rogers, R. ;"Why is evaluation research not utilized?" in Marcia Guttentag with Shalom Saar, ed., *Evaluation Studies Review Annual,* Volume 2, 1977 (Beverly Hills: Sage, 1977): 327-333.

Agency for International Development, *A.I.D. Use of Development Indicators: A Progress Report* (Washington, D.C.: Agency for International Development, 1974).

———— , *Evaluation Handbook* (Washington, D.C.: Agency for International Development, 1974).

Alkin, M. C. ;"Evaluation theory development," *Evaluation Comment* 2 (1969): 2-7.

Allison, G. T.,*Essence of Decision: Explaining the Cuban Missile Crisis* (Boston: Little, Brown, 1971).

Alwin, D. F. and M. J. Sullivan, "Issues of design and analysis in evaluation research," *Sociological Methods and Research* 4 (1975): 77-100.

Anderson, A. B. ;"Policy experiments: selected analytic issues," *Sociological Methods and Research* 4 (1975): 13-30.

Argyris, C. ;"Creating effective research relationships in organizations," *Human Organization* 17 (1958): 34-40.

Aronson, S. H. and C. C. Sherwood, "Researcher versus practitioner: problems in social action research," *Social Work* 12 (1967): 89-96.

Backstrom, C. H. and G. D. Hursh, *Survey Research* (Evanston, Ill.: Northwestern University Press, 1963).

Bauer, R. A., "Detection and anticipation of impact: the nature of the task," in Raymond A. Bauer, ed., *Social Indicators* (Cambridge, Mass.: M.I.T. Press, 1966): 1-67.

———— , ed., *Social Indicators* (Cambridge, Mass.: M.I.T. Press, 1966).

Beaglehole, E., "Evaluation techniques for induced technological change," *International Social Science Bulletin* 7 (1955): 376-386.

Becker, H. S. ;"Problems of inference and proof in participant observation," *American Sociological Review* 23 (1958): 652-660.

Belshaw, C. S. ;"Evaluation of technical assistance as a contribution to development," *International Development Review* 8 (1966): 2-23.

Bennett, C. A. and A. A. Lumsdaine, eds., *Evaluation and Experiment: Some Critical Issues in Assessing Social Programs* (New York: Academic Press, 1975).

_____ , "Social program evaluation: definitions and issues," in Carl A. Bennett and Arthur A. Lumsdaine, eds., *Evaluation and Experiment: Some Critical Issues in Assessing Social Programs* (New York: Academic Press, 1975): 1-38.

Berk, R. A. and P. H. Rossi, "Doing good or worse: evaluation research politically reexamined," *Social Problems* 23 (1976): 337-349.

Bernstein, I. N., ed., *Validity Issues in Evaluative Research* (Beverly Hills: Sage, 1976).

_____ , "Validity issues in evaluative research: an overview," *Sociological Methods and Research* 4 (1975): 3-12.

_____ , G. W. Bohrnstedt, and E. F. Borgatta, "External validity and evaluation research: a codification of problems," *Sociological Methods and Research* 4 (1975): 100-128.

Bernstein, I. N. and H. E. Freeman, *Academic and Entrepreneurial Research: The Consequences of Diversity in Federal Evaluation Studies* (New York: Russell Sage, 1975).

Biderman, A. D., "Anticipatory studies and stand-by research capabilities," in Raymond A. Bauer, ed., *Social Indicators* (Cambridge, Mass.: M.I.T. Press, 1966): 272-301.

_____ , "Social indicators and goals," in Raymond A. Bauer, ed., *Social Indicators* (Cambridge, Mass.: M.I.T. Press, 1966): 68-153.

Blalock, H. M., *Causal Models in the Social Sciences* (Chicago: Aldine, 1971).

Boruch, R. F. ,"Bibliography: illustrative randomized field experiments for planning and evaluation," mimeo, Evanston, Illinois, Northwestern University, 1974.

_____ , "Coupling randomized experiments and approximations to experiments in social program evaluation," *Sociological Methods and Research* 4 (1975): 31-53.

_____ , "On common contentions about randomized field experiments," in R. F. Boruch and H. W. Riecken, eds., *Experimental Testing of Public Policy: The Proceedings of the 1974 Social Science Research Council Conference on Social Experiments* (Boulder, Colorado: Westview, 1975): 107-142.

_____ , "Problems in research utilization: use of social experiments, experimental results and auxiliary data in experiments," *Annals of the New York Academy of Sciences* 218 (1973): 56-77.

_____ and H. W. Riecken, "Final report: applications of randomized experiments to planning and evaluating AID programs," unpublished paper, October, 1974.

Box, G.E.P. and G. M. Jenkins, *Time Series Analysis: Forecasting and Control* (San Francisco: Holden-Day, 1970).

Box, G.E.P. and G. C. Tiao, "A change in level of nonstationary time series," *Biometrika* 52 (1965): 181-192.

_____ , "Intervention analysis with applications to economic and environmental problems," *Journal of the American Statistical Association* 70 (1975): 70-79.

Brooks, M. P., "The community action program as a setting for applied research," *Journal of Social Issues* 21 (1965): 29-40.

Buse, A., "Goodness of fit in generalized least squares estimation," *American Statistician* 27 (1973): 106-108.

Caiden, N. and A. Wildavsky, *Planning and Budgeting in Poor Countries* (New York: John Wiley, 1974).

Cain, G. G., "Regression and selection models to improve nonexperimental comparisons," in Carl A. Bennett and Arthur A. Lumsdaine, eds., *Evaluation and Experiment: Some Critical Issues in Assessing Social Programs* (New York: Academic Press, 1975): 297-317.

_____ and R. G. Hollister, "The methodology of evaluating social action programs," in *Discussion Papers,* Institute for Research on Poverty, University of Wisconsin, Madison, Wisconsin, 1969.

Cain, G.C. and H.W. Watts, "Problems in making policy infererences from the Coleman report," *American Sociological Review* 35 (1970): 228-242.

Campbell, D.T., "Assessing the impact of planned social change, "in Gene M. Lyons, ed., *Social Research and Public Policies: The Dartmouth/OECD Conference* (Hanover, N.H.: University Press of New England, 1975): 3-45.

_____ , "Considering the case against experimental evaluations of social innovations," *Administrative Science Quarterly* 15 (1970): 110-113.

_____ , "Focal local indicators for social program evaluation," *Social Indicators Research* 3 (1976): 237-256.

_____ , "Methods for the experimenting society," *American Psychologist,* forthcoming.

_____ , "Reforms as experiments," *American Psychologist* 24 (1969): 409-429.

_____ and R. F. Boruch, "Making the case for randomized assignment to treatments by considering the alternatives: six ways in which quasi-experimental evaluations in compensatory education tend to underestimate effects," in C. A. Bennett and A. A. Lumsdaine, eds., *Evaluation and Experiment: Some Critical Issues in Assessing Social Programs* (New York: Academic Press, 1975): 195-296.

Campbell, D. T. and A. Erlebacher, "How regression artifacts in quasi-experimental evaluations can mistakenly make compensatory education look harmful," in J. Hellmuth, ed., *Compensatory Education: A National Debate,* Volume 3, *Disadvantaged Child* (New York: Brunner/Mazel, 1970): 185-210.

_____ , "Reply to the replies," in J. Hellmuth, ed., *Compensatory Education: A National Debate,* Volume 3, *Disadvantaged Child* (New York: Brunner/Mazel, 1970): 221-225.

Campbell, D. T. and H. L. Ross, "The Connecticut crackdown on speeding: time-series data in quasi-experimental analysis," *Law and Society Review* 3 (1968): 33-53.

Campbell, D. T. and J. C. Stanley, *Experimental and Quasi-Experimental Designs for Research* (Chicago: Rand McNally, 1963).

Caplan, N. ,"Factors associated with knowledge use among federal executives," *Policy Studies Journal* 4 (1976): 229-234.

_____ , "Social research and national policy: what gets used, by whom, for what purposes, and with what effects," in M. Guttentag with S. Saar, eds., *Evaluation Studies Review Annual,* Volume 2 (Beverly Hills: Sage, 1977): 351-359.

_____ , "The use of social science information by federal executives," in G. M. Lyons, ed., *Social Research and Public Policies: The Dartmouth/OECD Conference* (Hanover, N.H.: University Press of New England, 1975): 46-67.

Caporaso, J. A., "Quasi-experimental approaches to social science: perspectives and problems," in J. A. Caporaso and L. L. Roos, Jr., eds., *Quasi-Experimental Approaches: Testing Theory and Evaluating Policy* (Evanston, Ill.: Northwestern University Press, 1973): 3-38.

_____ , and Leslie L. Roos, Jr., eds., *Quasi-Experimental Approaches: Testing Theory and Evaluating Policy* (Evanston, Ill.: Northwestern University Press, 1973).

Caro, F. G.,"Evaluation in comprehensive urban antipoverty programs: a case study of an attempt to establish the evaluative research role in a model city program," in F. G. Caro, ed., *Readings in Evaluation Research* (New York: Russell Sage, 1971): 297-317.

_____ , "Evaluation research: an overview," in F. G. Caro, ed., *Readings in Evaluation Research* (New York: Russell Sage, 1971): 1-34.

_____ , ed., *Readings in Evaluation Research* (New York: Russell Sage, 1971).

Chapin, F. S.,"An experiment on the social effects of good housing," *American Sociological Review* 5 (1940): 868-879.

Chow, G. C., "Tests of equality between sets of coefficients in two linear regressions," *Econometrica* 28 (1960): 591-605.

Cicarelli, V.,"The impact of Head Start: executive summary," in *The Impact of Head Start: An Evaluation of the Effects of Head Start on Children's Cognitive and Affective Development,* Volume 1 (Bladensburg, Maryland: Westinghouse Learning Corporation, 1969): 1-11.

_____ , "The relevance of the regression artifact problem to the Westinghouse-Ohio University evaluation of Head Start: a reply to Campbell and Erlebacher," in J. Hellmuth, ed., *Compensatory Education: A National Debate,* Volume 3, *Disadvantaged Child* (New York: Brunner/Mazel, 1970): 211-215.

Cohen, D. K., "Politics and research: evaluation of social action programs in education," *Review of Educational Research* 40 (1970): 213-238.

Cohen, J.,"Multiple regression as a general data-analytic system," in Elmer L. Struening and Marcia Guttentag, eds., *Handbook of Evaluation Research,* Volume 1 (Beverly Hills: Sage, 1975): 571-595.

Cohen, M. R. and E. Nagel, *An Introduction to Logic and Scientific Method* (New York: Harcourt, Brace, 1934).

Coleman, J. S., "Evaluating educational programs," *Urban Review* 3 (1969): 6-8.

_____ , "Reply to Cain and Watts," *American Sociological Review* 35 (1970): 228-242.

Cook, T. D., "Sesame Street and the medical and tailored models of summative evaluation research," in J. Abert and M. Kamrass, eds., *Social Experiments and Social Program Evaluation* (Cambridge, Mass.: Ballinger, 1974): 28-37.

_____ , "The potential and limitations of secondary evaluations," in M. W. Apple, M. J. Subkoviak, and H. S. Lufler, Jr., eds., *Educational Evaluation: Analysis and Responsibility* (Berkeley: McCutchan, 1974): 155-222.

_____ and D. T. Campbell, "The design and conduct of quasi-experiments and true experiments in field settings," in M. D. Dunnette, ed., *Handbook of Industrial and Organizational Research* (Chicago: Rand McNally, 1975): 223-326.

Cook, T. D. and R. F. Conner, "The educational impact," *Journal of Communication* 26 (1976): 155-164.

Cook, T. D., F. L. Cook, and M. M. Mark, "Randomized and quasi-experimental designs in evaluation research: an introduction," in L. Rutman, ed., *Evaluation Research Methods: A Basic Guide* (Beverly Hills: Sage, 1977): 103-140.

Cook, T. D. and C. L. Gruder, "Metaevaluation research," *Evaluation Quarterly,* forthcoming.

Cook, T. D. and W. E. Pollard, "How to recognize and avoid some common problems of misutilization of evaluation research findings," *Evaluation,* forthcoming.

Cook, T. D. and C. S. Reichardt, "Guidelines: statistical analysis of non-equivalent control group designs: a guide to some current literature," *Evaluation* 3 (1976): 136-138.

Cook, T. J. and F. P. Scioli, Jr., "A research strategy for analyzing the impacts of public policy," *Administrative Science Quarterly* 17 (1972): 328-339.

Cooley, W.W. and P.R. Lohnes, *Multivariate Data Analysis* (New York: John Wiley, 1971).

Cox, G. B., "Managerial style: implications for the utilization of program evaluation information," *Evaluation Quarterly* 1 (1977): 499-508.

Crecine, J. P., *Governmental Problem Solving: A Computer Simulation of Municipal Budgeting* (Chicago: Rand McNally, 1969).

Datta, L.-E., "Does it work when it has been tried? and half full or half empty?" *Journal of Career Education* 2 (1976): 38-55.

Davies, J. C., III, "Measuring the social costs of technological and environmental change," in G. M. Lyons, ed., *Social Research and Public Policies: The Dartmouth/OECD Conference* (Hanover, N.H.: University Press of New England, 1975): 68-84.

Davis, H. R. and S. E. Salasin, "Applied social research: in combat with waste and suffering," in M. Guttentag with S. Saar, eds., *Evaluation Studies Review Annual,* Volume 2 (Beverly Hills: Sage, 1977): 320-326.

Deutsch, K. W., *The Nerves of Government* (New York: Free Press, 1963).

Dexter, L. A., *Elite and Specialized Interviewing* (Evanston, Ill.: Northwestern University Press, 1970).

Diaz-Guerrero, R. and W. H. Holtzman, "Learning by televised 'Plaza Sesamo' in Mexico," *Journal of Educational Psychology* 66 (1974): 632-643.

Diaz-Guerrero, R., I. Reyes-Lagunes, D. B. Witzke, and W. H. Holtzman, "Plaza Sesamo in Mexico: an evaluation," *Journal of Communication* 26 (1976): 155-164.

Downs, A., "Some thoughts on giving people economic advice," *American Behavioral Scientist* 9 (1965): 30-32.

Durbin, J. and G. S. Watson, "Testing for serial correlation in least squares regression," Part I, *Biometrika* 37 (1950): 409-428.

———, "Testing for serial correlation in least squares regression," Part II, *Biometrika* 38 (1951): 159-178.

Dye, T. R. and N. F. Pollack, "Path analytic models in policy research," in F. P. Scioli and T. J. Cook, eds., *Methodologies for Analyzing Public Policies* (Lexington, Mass.: Lexington Books, 1975): 113-122.

Eber, H. W., "Multivariate methodologies for evaluation research," in E. L. Struening and M. Guttentag, eds., *Handbook of Evaluation Research,* Volume 1 (Beverly Hills: Sage, 1975): 553-570.

Edwards, W. and M. Guttentag, "Experiments and evaluations: a reexamination," in C. A. Bennett and A. A. Lumsdaine, eds., *Evaluation and Experiment: Some Critical Issues in Assessing Social Programs* (New York: Academic Press, 1975): 409-463.

_____ and K. Snapper, "A decision-theoretic approach to evaluation research," in E. L. Struening and M. Guttentag, eds., *Handbook of Evaluation Research,* Volume 1 (Beverly Hills: Sage, 1975): 139-181.

Effectiveness Auditing in Government Administration, Goals and Methods for Examining the Effectiveness of Central Government in Sweden: Summary of a Report of the Swedish National Audit Bureau 1970, The Swedish National Audit Bureau.

Elinson, J. "Effectiveness of social action programs in health and welfare," in Abraham Bergman, ed., *Assessing the Effectiveness of Child Health Services: Report of the Forty-Sixth Ross Conference on Pediatric Research* (Columbus, Ohio: Ross Laboratories, 1976): 77-81.

Evans, J. W., "Head Start: comments on the criticism," in D. G. Hays, ed., *Britannica Review of American Education,* Volume 1 (Chicago: Encyclopedia Britannica, 1969): 253-260.

_____ and J. Schiller, "How preoccupation with possible regression artifacts can lead to a faulty strategy for the evaluation of social action programs: a reply to Campbell and Erlebacher," in J. Hellmuth, ed., *Compensatory Education: A National Debate,* Volume 3, *Disadvantaged Child* (New York: Brunner/Mazel, 1970): 216-220.

Fairweather, K., *Methods for Experimental Social Innovation* (New York: John Wiley, 1967).

Franklin, J. L. and J. H. Thrasher, *An Introduction to Program Evaluation* (New York: John Wiley, 1976).

Freedman, R. "The research challenge to social scientists in the developing family planning programs: the case of Taiwan," *Journal of Social Issues* 23 (1967): 165-169.

_____ and J. Y. Takeshita, *Family Planning in Taiwan: An Experiment in Social Change* (Princeton, N.J.: Princeton University Press, 1969).

Freeman, H. E., "Evaluation research and public policies," in G. M. Lyons, ed., *Social Research and Public Policies: The Dartmouth/OECD Conference* (Hanover, N.H.: University Press of New England, 1975): 141-174.

_____, "The present status of evaluation research,' in M. Guttentag with S. Saar, eds., *Evaluation Studies Review Annual,* Volume 2 (Beverly Hills: Sage, 1977): 17-51.

_____ and C. C. Sherwood, "Research in large-scale intervention programs," *Journal of Social Issues* 21 (1965): 11-28.

_____ , *Social Research and Social Policy* (Englewood Cliffs, N.J.: Prentice-Hall, 1970).

Glass, G. V., "Estimating the effects of intervention into a non-stationary time-series," *American Educational Research Journal* 9 (1972): 463-477.

———, ed., *Evaluation Studies Review Annual,* Volume 1 (Beverly Hills: Sage, 1976).

———, G. C. Tiao, and T. O. Maguire, "The 1900 revision of German divorce laws: analysis of data as a time-series quasi-experiment," *Law and Society Review* 5 (1971): 539-562.

Glass, G. V., V. L. Wilson, and J. M. Gottman, *Design and Analysis of Time-Series Experiments* (Boulder: Colorado Associated University Press, 1975).

Gilbert, J. P., R. J. Light, and F. Mosteller, "Assessing social innovations: an empirical base for policy," in C. A. Bennett and A. A. Lumsdaine, eds., *Evaluation and Experiment: Some Critical Issues in Assessing Social Programs* (New York: Academic Press, 1975): 39-193.

Glennan, T. K., Jr., *Evaluating Federal Manpower Programs: Notes and Observations,* RAND Corporation Memorandum, RM-5743-OEO, Santa Monica, California, 1969.

Goldberger, A. S. and O. D. Duncan, ed., *Structural Equation Models in the Social Sciences* (New York: Seminar Press, 1973).

Goodwin, L., "Social experiments and policy research," *Policy Studies Journal* 5 (1976): 244-250.

Greenburg, B. G., "Evaluation of social programs," *Review of the International Statistical Institute* 36 (1968): 260-277.

Gross, B. M., "Management strategy for economic and social development: part I," *Policy Sciences* 2 (1971): 339-371.

———, "Management strategy for economic and social development: part II," *Policy Sciences* 3 (1972): 1-25.

———, "The state of the nation: social systems accounting," in R. A. Bauer, ed., *Social Indicators* (Cambridge, Mass.: M.I.T. Press, 1966): 154-271.

Guba, E. G., "The failure of educational evaluation," *Educational Technology* 9 (1969): 29-38.

Gujarti, D., "Use of dummy variables in testing equality between sets of coefficients in two linear regressions: a note," *American Statistician* 24, 4 (1970): 50-52.

———, "Use of dummy variables in testing for equality between sets of coefficients in linear regressions: a generalization," *American Statistician* 24, 5 (1970): 18-22.

Gurel, L., "The human side of evaluating human services programs: problems and prospects," in M. Guttentag and E. L. Struening, eds., *Handbook of Evaluation Research,* Volume 2 (Beverly Hills: Sage, 1975): 11-28.

Gurr, T. R., *Politimetrics: An Introduction to Quantitative Macropolitics* (Englewood Cliffs, N.J.: Prentice-Hall, 1972).

Guttentag, M., "An approach to evaluation," unpublished paper SHC.75/WS/3, Paris, United Nations Educational, Scientific and Cultural Organization, February 3, 1975.

———, "Evaluation and society," *Personality and Social Psychology Bulletin* 3 (1977): 31-40.

———, "Evaluation of social intervention programs," *Annals of the New York Academy of Sciences* 218 (1973): 3-13.

———, "Subjectivity and its use in evaluation research," *Evaluation* 1 (1973): 60-65.

_____ with S. Saar, eds., *Evaluation Studies Review Annual*, Volume 2 (Beverly Hills: Sage, 1977),

Guttentag, M. and K. Snapper, "Plans, evaluations, and decisions," *Evaluation* 2 (1974): 58-64, 73-74.

Guttentag, M. and E. L. Struening, eds., *Handbook of Evaluation Research*, Volume 2 (Beverly Hills: Sage, 1975).

Hayes, S. P., Jr., *Evaluating Development Projects* (Paris: United Nations Educational, Scientific and Cultural Organization, 1966).

Hays, W. L., *Statistics for Psychologists* (New York: Holt, Rinehart and Winston, 1963).

Hibbs, D. A., Jr., "On analyzing the effects of policy interventions: Box-Jenkins and Box-Tiao vs. structural equation models," in D. Heise, ed., *Sociological Methodology 1977* (San Francisco: Jossey-Bass, 1977): 137-179.

_____ , "Political parties and macroeconomic policy," *American Political Science Review* 71 (1977): 1467-1487.

_____ , "Problems of statistical estimation and causal inference in time-series regression models," in H. L. Costner, ed., *Sociological Methodology 1973-1974* (San Francisco: Jossey-Bass, 1974): 252-308.

Higgins, B. "The evaluation of technical assistance," *International Journal* 25 (1969-1970): 34-55.

Hilton, E. T. and A. A. Lumsdaine, "Field trial designs in gauging the impact of fertility planning programs," in C. A. Bennett and A. A. Lumsdaine, eds., *Evaluation and Experiment: Some Critical Issues in Assessing Social Programs* (New York: Academic Press, 1975): 319-408.

Holsti, O. R., *Content Analysis for the Social Sciences and Humanities* (Reading, Mass.: Addison-Wesley, 1969).

Hoole, F. W., "Evaluating the impact of international organizations," *International Organization* 31 (1977): 541-563.

_____ , *Politics and Budgeting in the World Health Organization* (Bloomington, Indiana: Indiana University Press, 1976).

_____ , "The behavioral science orientation to the study of international administration," in R. S. Jordan, ed., *Multinational Cooperation: Economic, Social, and Scientific Development* (New York: Oxford University Press, 1972): 327-364.

_____ , B. L. Job, and H. J. Tucker, "Incremental budgeting and international organizations," *American Journal of Political Science* 20 (1976): 273-301.

Hoole, F. W. and D. A. Zinnes, eds., *Quantitative International Politics: An Appraisal* (New York: Praeger, 1976).

Houston, T. R., Jr., "The behavioral sciences impact-effectiveness model," in P. H. Rossi and W. Williams, eds., *Evaluating Social Programs: Theory, Practice and Politics* (New York: Seminar Press, 1972): 51-65.

Hultin, M., "Evaluation of education projects financed by the World Bank group," in C. C. Abt, ed., *The Evaluation of Social Programs* (Beverly Hills: Sage, 1977): 407-413.

Jahoda, M. and E. Barnitz, "The nature of evaluation," *International Social Science Bulletin* 7 (1955): 353-364.

James, J. L., ed., "Symposium on introductory textbooks on public policy analysis," *Policy Studies Journal* 5 (1976): 250-262.

Johnson, R. W. and J. M. Pierce, "The economic evaluation of policy impacts: cost-benefit and cost-effectiveness analysis," in F. P. Scioli, Jr. and T. J. Cook, eds., *Methodologies for Analyzing Public Policies* (Lexington, Mass.: Lexington Books, 1975): 131-154.

Johnston, J., *Econometric Methods* (Tokyo: McGraw-Hill Kugakusha, 1972).

Katz, D. ;"Feedback in social systems: operational and systemic research on production, maintenance, control and adaptive functions," in C. A. Bennett and A. A. Lumsdaine, eds., *Evaluation and Experiment: Some Critical Issues in Assessing Social Programs* (New York: Academic Press, 1975): 465-523.

Kerlinger, F. N., *Foundations of Behavioral Research: Educational and Psychological Inquiry* (New York: Holt, Rinehart and Winston, 1966).

Kershaw, D. N., "Issues in income maintenance experimentation," in P. H. Rossi and W. Williams, eds., *Evaluating Social Programs: Theory, Practice and Politics* (New York: Seminar Press, 1972): 221-245.

_____ , "The New Jersey negative income tax experiment: a summary of the design, operations and results of the first large-scale social science experiment," in G. M. Lyons, ed., *Social Research and Public Policies: The Dartmouth/ OECD Conference* (Hanover, N.H.: University Press of New England, 1975): 87-116.

Klineberg, O., "The problem of evaluation," *International Social Science Bulletin* 7 (1955): 345-352.

Kmenta, J., *Elements of Econometrics* (New York: Macmillan, 1971).

Land, K. C. and S. Spilerman, eds., *Social Indicator Models* (New York: Russell Sage, 1975).

Lemieux, P. H., "Box-Jenkins models, quasi-experimental designs, and forecasting in international relations," paper prepared for delivery at the Annual Meetings of the International Studies Association, Royal York Hotel, Toronto, Canada, February 25-29, 1976.

Leonard, W. R., B. A. Jenny, and O. Nwali, *UN Development Aid: Criteria and Methods of Evaluation* (New York: Arno Press, 1971).

Lerman, P. ;"Evaluative studies of institutions for delinquents: implications for research and social policy," *Social Work* 13 (1968): 55-64.

Levin, H. M., "Cost-effectiveness analysis in evaluation research," in M. Guttentag and E. L. Struening, eds., *Handbook of Evaluation Research,* Volume 2 (Beverly Hills: Sage, 1975): 89-122.

Levine, A. and M. Levine, "The social context of evaluation research: a case study," *Evaluation Quarterly* 1 (1977): 515-542.

Levitan, S. A., "Evaluating social programs," *Society* 14 (1977): 66-68.

Lindblom, C.E., "The science of muddling through," *Public Administration Review* 19 (1959): 79-88.

Lipsky, M. ;"Views on the American experience with social experimentation: perspectives from conference discussion," in G. M. Lyons, ed., *Social Research and Public Policies: The Dartmouth/OECD Conference* (Hanover, N. H.: University Press of New England, 1975): 131-138.

Longwood, R. and A. Simmel, "Organizational resistance to innovation suggested by research," in C. H. Weiss, ed., *Evaluating Action Programs: Readings in Social Action and Education* (Boston: Allyn and Bacon, 1972): 311-317.

Lumsdaine, A. A. and C. A. Bennett, "Assessing alternative conceptions of evaluation," in C. A. Bennett and A. A. Lumsdaine, eds., *Evaluation and Experiment: Some Critical Issues in Assessing Social Programs* (New York: Academic Press, 1975): 525-553.

Lyall, K. C., "Some observations on design issues in large-scale social experiments," *Sociological Methods and Research* 4 (1975): 54-77.

Lyden, F.J. and E.G. Miller, eds., *Planning, Programming, Budgeting: A Systems Approach to Management* (Chicago: Markham, 1972).

Lynn, L. E., Jr., "Policy relevant social research: what does it look like?" in M. Guttentag with S. Saar, eds., *Evaluation Studies Review Annual,* Volume 2 (Beverly Hills: Sage, 1977): 63-76.

Lyons, G. M., ed., *Social Research and Public Policies: The Dartmouth/OECD Conference* (Hanover, N.H.: University Press of New England, 1975).

Mann, F. and R. Likert, "The need for research on the communication of research results," *Human Organization* 11 (1952): 15-19.

Mann, J. ,"Technical and social difficulties in the conduct of evaluative research," in J. Mann, *Changing Human Behavior* (New York: Charles Scribner's Sons, 1965): 177-189.

_____ , "The outcome of evaluative research," in C. H. Weiss, ed., *Evaluating Action Programs: Readings in Social Action and Education* (Boston: Allyn and Bacon, 1972): 267-282.

McCain, L. J., R. McCleary, and T. D. Cook, "The statistical analysis of interrupted time-series quasi-experiments," in T. D. Cook and D. T. Campbell, eds., *The Design and Analysis of Quasi-Experiments in Field Settings* (Chicago: Rand McNally, forthcoming).

McDill, E. L., M. S. McDill, and J. T. Sprehe, "Evaluation in practice: compensatory education," in P. H. Rossi and W. Williams, eds., *Evaluating Social Programs: Theory, Practice and Politics* (New York: Seminar Press, 1972): 141-185.

Miller, K. M., "Evaluation in adult education," *International Social Science Bulletin* 7 (1955): 430-442.

Miller, W. B., "The impact of a 'total community' delinquency control project," *Social Problems* 10 (1962): 186-191.

Montgomery, J. D. and M. Katzman, "Cui Buno? measuring income-redistribution effects of capital projects," in M. Guttentag with S. Saar, eds., *Evaluation Studies Review Annual,* Volume 2 (Beverly Hills: Sage, 1977): 181-194.

Moss, L., "A meeting on criteria and techniques of evaluation of technical assistance for economic development," *International Social Science Bulletin* 7 (1955): 443-458.

_____ , "The evaluation of fundamental education," *International Social Science Bulletin* 7 (1955): 398-417.

Moursund, J. P., *Evaluation: An Introduction to Research Design* (Monterey, Ca.: Brooks/Cole, 1973).

Nagel, S. S. with M. Neef, *Operations Research Methods: As Applied to Political Science and the Legal Process* (Beverly Hills :Sage, 1976).

Naylor, T. H., ed., *Computer Simulation Experiments with Models of Economic Systems* (New York: John Wiley, 1971).

_____ , T. G. Seaks, and D. W. Wichern, "Box-Jenkins methods: an alternative to econometric models," *International Statistics Review* 40 (1972): 123-137.

Nelson, C.R., *Applied Time Series Analysis for Managerial Forecasting* (San Francisco: Holden-Day, 1970).

Nielsen, V. G., "Input-output models and the nonuse of policy analysis," in M. J. White, M. Radnor, and D. A. Tansik, eds., *Management and Policy Science in American Government* (Lexington, Mass.: Lexington Books, 1975): 195-203.

Noble, J. H., Jr., "The limits of cost-benefit analysis as a guide to priority-setting in rehabilitation," *Evaluation Quarterly* 1 (1977): 347-380.

Nunnally, J. C. and R. L. Durham, "Validity, reliability, and special problems of measurement in evaluation research," in E. L. Struening and M. Guttentag, eds., *Handbook of Evaluation Research,* Volume 1 (Beverly Hills: Sage, 1975): 289-352.

Nunnally, J. C. and W. H. Wilson, "Method and theory for developing measures in evaluation research," in E.L. Struening and M. Guttentag, eds., *Handbook of Evaluation Research,* Volume 1 (Beverly Hills: Sage, 1975): 227-288.

Organization for Economic Cooperation and Development, *The Evaluation of Technical Assistance* (Paris: Organization for Economic Cooperation and Development, 1969).

Pan Lu, L., H. C. Chen, and L. P. Chow, "An experimental study of the effect of group meetings on the acceptance of family planning in Taiwan," *Journal of Social Issues* 23 (1967): 171-177.

Perkins, D. N. T., "Evaluating social interventions: a conceptual schema," *Evaluation Quarterly* 1 (1977): 639-656.

Peterson, R. E. and K. K. Seo, "Public administration planning in developing countries: a bayesian decision theory approach," *Policy Sciences* 3 (1972): 371-378.

Porter, A. C. and T. R. Chibucos, "Common problems of design and analysis in evaluative research," *Sociological Methods and Research* 3 (1975): 235-257.

Pressman, J. L., "Decisionmakers and evaluators: some differences in perspective and possible directions for the future," in G. M. Lyons, ed., *Social Research and Public Policies: The Dartmouth/OECD Conference* (Hanover, N.H.: University Press of New England, 1975): 198-205.

_____ and A. B. Wildavsky, *Implementation* (Berkeley: University of California Press, 1973).

Reichardt, C. S.,"The statistical analysis of data from the nonequivalent control group design," in T. D. Cook and D. T. Campbell, eds., *The Design and Analysis of Quasi-Experiments in Field Settings* (Chicago: Rand McNally, forthcoming).

Riecken, H. W., "Memorandum on program evaluation," in C. H. Weiss, ed., *Evaluating Action Programs: Readings in Social Action and Education* (Boston: Allyn and Bacon, 1972): 85-104.

_____, R. F. Boruch, D. T. Campbell, N. Caplan, T. K. Glennan, Jr., J. W. Pratt, A. Rees, and W. Williams, *Social Experimentation: A Method for Planning and Evaluating Social Intervention* (New York: Academic Press, 1974).

Rivlin, A. M., "Allocating resources for policy research: how can experiments be more useful?" *American Economic Review* 64 (1974): 346-354.

_____, *Systematic Thinking for Social Action* (Washington, D.C.: Brookings Institution, 1971).

Rodman, H. and R. Kolodny, "Organizational strains in the researcher-practitioner relationship," *Human Organization* 23 (1964): 171-182.

Roman, D. D., "The PERT system: an appraisal of program evaluation review technique," in H. C. Schulberg, A. Sheldon, and F. Baker, eds., *Program*

Evaluation in the Health Fields (New York: Behavioral Publications, 1969): 243-253.

Rooks, D. C., *PERT, program evaluation and review technique, 1962-1974: An Annotated Bibliography,* Council of Planning Librarians Exchange Bibliography 958 (Monticello, Ill.: Council of Planning Librarians, 1976).

Roos, L. L., Jr., "Panels, rotation, and events," in J. A. Caporaso and L. L. Roos, Jr., eds., *Quasi-Experimental Approaches: Testing Theory and Evaluating Policy* (Evanston, Ill.: Northwestern University Press, 1973): 39-92.

_____ , "Quasi-experiments and environmental policy," *Policy Sciences* 6 (1975): 249-265.

Roos, N. P., "Contrasting social experimentation with retrospective evaluation: a health care perspective," *Public Policy* 23 (1975): 241-257.

_____ , "Evaluation, quasi-experimentation, and public policy," in J. A. Caporaso and L. L. Roos, Jr., eds., *Quasi-Experimental Approaches: Testing Theory and Evaluating Policy* (Evanston, Ill.:NorthwesternUniversity Press, 1973): 281-304.

Rosenthal, R. A. and R. S. Weiss, "Problems of organizational feedback processes," in R. A. Bauer, ed., *Social Indicators* (Cambridge, Mass.: M.I.T. Press, 1966): 302-340.

Ross, H. L., D. T. Campbell, and G. V. Glass, "Determining the social effects of a legal reform: the British 'breathalyser' crackdown of 1967," *American Behavioral Scientist* 13 (1970): 493-509.

Rossi, P. H., "Boobytraps and pitfalls in the evaluation of social action programs," *Proceedings of the Social Statistics Section* (Washington, D.C.: American Statistical Association, 1966): 127-132.

_____ , "Evaluating educational programs," *Urban Review* 3 (1969): 17-18.

_____ , "Evaluating social action programs," in F. G. Caro, ed., *Readings in Evaluation Research* (New York: Russell Sage, 1971): 276-281.

_____ , "Field experiments in social programs: problems and prospects," in G. M. Lyons, ed., *Social Research and Public Policies: The Dartmouth/OECD Conference* (Hanover, N.H.: University Press of New England, 1975): 117-130.

_____ , "Observations on the organization of social research," in P. H. Rossi and W. Williams, eds., *Evaluating Social Programs: Theory, Practice and Politics* (New York: Seminar Press, 1972): 267-286.

_____ , "Testing for success and failure in social action," in P. H. Rossi and W. Williams, eds., *Evaluating Social Programs: Theory, Practice and Politics* (New York: Seminar Press, 1972): 11-49.

_____ and W. Williams, eds., *Evaluating Social Programs: Theory, Practice and Politics* (New York: Seminar Press, 1972).

Rossi, P. H. and S. R. Wright, "Evaluation research: an assessment of theory, practice, and politics," *Evaluation Quarterly* 1 (1977): 5-52.

Rothenberg, J. ,"Cost-benefit analysis: a methodological exposition," in M. Guttentag and E. L. Struening, eds., *Handbook of Evaluation Research,* Volume 2 (Beverly Hills: Sage, 1975): 55-88.

Rudner, S., *Philosophy of Social Science* (Englewood Cliffs, N.J.: Prentice-Hall, 1966).

Rummel, R. J., "Understanding factor analysis," *Journal of Conflict Resolution* 11 (1967): 444-480.

Russett, B. M., H. R. Alker, Jr., K. W. Deutsch, and H. Lasswell, *World Handbook of Political and Social Indicators* (New Haven, Conn.: Yale University Press, 1964).

Schulberg, H. C. and F. Baker, "Program evaluation models and the implementation of research findings," *American Journal of Public Health* 58 (1968): 1248-1255.

Schulberg, H. C., A. Sheldon, and F. Baker, *Program Evaluation in the Health Fields* (New York: Behavioral Publications, 1970).

Schultze, C. L., *The Politics and Economics of Public Spending* (Washington, D.C.: Brookings Institution, 1968).

Scioli, F. P., Jr. and T. J. Cook, eds., *Methodologies for Analyzing Public Policies* (Lexington, Mass.: Lexington Books, 1975).

Scriven, M., "Evaluation bias and its control," in G. V. Glass, ed., *Evaluation Studies Review Annual,* Volume 1 (Beverly Hills: Sage, 1976): 119-139.

———, "Evaluating educational programs," *Urban Review* 3 (1969): 20-22.

———, "The methodology of evaluation," in C. H. Weiss, ed., *Evaluating Action Programs: Readings in Social Action and Education* (Boston: Allyn and Bacon, 1972): 123-136.

Selltiz, C. and E. Barnitz, "The evaluation of intergroup relations programmes," *International Social Science Bulletin* 7 (1955): 364-375.

Selltiz, C., M. Jahoda, M. Deutsch, and S. W. Cook, *Research Methods in Social Relations* (New York: Holt, Rinehart, and Winston, 1962).

Sheldon, E. B., "Social experimentation: a challenge for the seventies," in *Evaluating Government Performance: Changes and Challenges for GAO* (Washington, D.C.: U.S. Government Printing Office, 1975): 199-211.

——— and W. E. Moore, eds., *Indicators of Social Change* (New York: Russell Sage, 1968).

Sjoberg, G., "Politics, ethics and evaluation research," in M. Guttentag and E. L. Struening, eds., *Handbook of Evaluation Research,* Volume 2 (Beverly Hills: Sage, 1975): 29-51.

Skipper, J. K., Jr. and R. C. Leonard, "Children, stress, and hospitalization: a field experiment," *Journal of Health and Social Behavior* 9 (1968): 275-287.

Smith, B., "Evaluation of exchange of persons," *International Social Science Bulletin* 7 (1955): 387-397.

Stake, R. E., "The countenance of educational evaluation," *Teachers College Record* 68 (1967): 523-540.

Stanley, J. C., "Controlled field experiments as a model for evaluation," in P. H. Rossi and W. Williams, eds., *Evaluating Social Programs: Theory, Practice and Politics* (New York: Seminar Press, 1972): 67-71.

Steiber, S. R., *Evaluation Research: A Bibliographic Overview,* Council of Planning Librarians Exchange Bibliography 975 (Monticello, Ill.: Council of Planning Librarians, 1976).

Steinbruner, J., *The Cybernetic Theory of Decision: New Dimensions of Political Analysis* (Princeton, N.J.: Princeton University Press, 1974).

Stephan, A. S., "Prospects and Possibilities: The New Deal and The New Social Research," *Social Forces* 13 (1935): 515-521.

Stockton, R. S., *Introduction to Linear Programming* (Homewood, Ill.: Richard D. Irwin, 1971).

Struening, E. L. and M. Guttentag, eds., *Handbook of Evaluation Research,* Volume 1 (Beverly Hills: Sage, 1975).

Stycos, J. M. and K. W. Black, *The Control of Human Fertility in Jamaica* (Ithaca,

N.Y.: Cornell University Press, 1964).

Suchman, E.A., "Action for what? a critique of evaluative research," in C.H. Weiss, ed., *Evaluating Action Programs: Readings in Social Action and Education* (Boston: Allyn and Bacon, 1972): 52-84.

———, "Evaluating educational programs," *Urban Review* 3 (1969): 15-17.

———, *Evaluative Research: Principles and Practice in Public Service and Social Action Programs* (New York: Russell Sage, 1967).

Sullivan, W. G. and W. W. Claycombe, *Fundamentals of Forecasting* (Reston, Virginia: Reston, 1977).

Theil, H. and A. G. Nagar, "Testing the independence of regression disturbances," *Journal of the American Statistical Association* 56 (1961): 793-806.

Trow, M. ,"Methodological problems in the evaluation of innovation," in F. G. Caro, ed., *Readings in Evaluation Research* (New York: Russell Sage, 1971): 81-94.

Twain, D., "Developing and implementing a research strategy," in M. Guttentag and E. L. Struening, eds., *Handbook of Evaluation Research,* Volume 2 (Beverly Hills: Sage, 1975): 27-52.

United Nations, *A Study of the Capacity of the United Nations Development System,* Volumes 1 and 2 (Geneva: United Nations, 1969).

———, *Statistical Yearbook* (New York: United Nations, annually since 1948).

Van Meter, D. S. and H. B. Asher, "Causal perspectives on policy analysis," in F. P. Scioli and T. J. Cook, eds., *Methodologies for Analyzing Public Policies* (Lexington, Mass.: Lexington Books, 1975): 61-72.

Ward, D. A. and G. G. Kassebaum, "On biting the hand that feeds: some implications of sociological evaluations of correctional effectiveness," in C. H. Weiss, ed., *Evaluating Action Programs: Readings in Social Action and Education* (Boston: Allyn and Bacon, 1972): 300-310.

Watts, H. W., "Graduated work incentives: an experiment in negative taxation," *American Economic Review* 59 (1969): 463-472.

Webb, E. J., D. T. Campbell, R. D. Schwartz, and L. Sechrest, *Unobtrusive Measures: Nonreactive Research in the Social Sciences* (Chicago: Rand McNally, 1966).

Weinstein, A. S., "Evaluation through medical records and related information systems," in E. L. Struening and M. Guttentag, eds., *Handbook of Evaluation Research,* Volume 1 (Beverly Hills: Sage, 1975): 397-481.

Weiss, C. H., "Between the cup and the lip . . ." *Evaluation* 1 (1973): 49-55.

———, ed., *Evaluating Action Programs: Readings in Social Action and Education* (Boston: Allyn and Bacon, 1972).

———, "Evaluating educational and social action programs: a treeful of owls," in C. H. Weiss, ed., *Evaluating Action Programs: Readings in Social Action and Education* (Boston: Allyn and Bacon, 1972): 3-28.

———, "Evaluation research in the political context," in E. L. Struening and M. Guttentag, eds., *Handbook of Evaluation Research,* Volume 1 (Beverly Hills: Sage, 1975): 13-26.

———, *Evaluation Research: Methods of Assessing Program Effectiveness* (Englewood Cliffs, N.J.: Prentice-Hall, 1972).

———, "Interviewing in evaluation research," in E. R. Struening and M. Guttentag, eds., *Handbook of Evaluation Research,* Volume 1 (Beverly Hills: Sage, 1975): 355-395.

———, "Policy research in the university: practical aid or academic exercise?" *Policy Studies Journal* 4 (1976): 224-228.

———, "The meaning of research utilization," Paper prepared for the American

Society for Public Administration Meeting, Washington, D.C., April 21, 1976.

———, "The politicization of evaluation research," *Journal of Social Issues* 26 (1970): 57-68.

———, "Utilization of evaluation: toward comparative study," in U.S. House of Representatives, Committee on Government Operations, Research and Technical Programs Subcommittee, *The Use of Social Research in Federal Domestic Programs,* Volume 3 (Washington, D.C.: Government Printing Office, 1967): 426-432.

———, "Where politics and evaluation research meet," *Evaluation* 1 (1973): 37-45.

Weiss, J. A., "Using social science for social policy," *Policy Studies Journal* 4 (1976): 234-238.

Weiss, R. S. and M. Rein, "The evaluation of broad-aim programs: a cautionary case and a moral," *Annals of the American Academy of Political and Social Science* 385 (1969): 133-142.

———, "The evaluation of broad-aim programs: difficulties in experimental design and an alternative," in C. H. Weiss, ed., *Evaluating Action Programs: Readings in Social Action and Education* (Boston: Allyn and Bacon, 1972): 236-249.

———, "The evaluation of broad-aid programs: experimental design, its difficulties, and an alternative," *Administrative Science Quarterly* 15 (1970): 97-109.

Wheelwright, S. C. and S. Makridakis, *Forecasting Methods for Management* (New York: John Wiley, 1977).

Wholey, J. S., "The role of evaluation and the evaluator in improving public programs: the bad news, the good news, and a bicentennial challenge," *Public Administration Review* 36 (1976): 679-683.

———, "What can we actually get from program evaluation," *Policy Sciences* 3 (1972): 361-369.

———, H. G. Duffy, J. S. Fukumoto, J. W. Scanlon, M. A. Berlin, W. C. Copeland, and J. G. Zelinsky, "Proper organizational relationships," in Carol H. Weiss, ed., *Evaluating Action Programs: Readings in Social Action and Education* (Boston: Allyn and Bacon, 1972): 118-122.

Wholey, J. S., J. N. Nay, J. W. Scanlon, and R. E. Schmidt, "Evaluation: when is it really needed?" *Evaluation* 2 (1975): 89-93.

———, "If you don't care where you get to, then it doesn't matter which way you go," in G. M. Lyons, ed., *Social Research and Public Policies: The Dartmouth/OECD Conference* (Hanover, N.H.: University Press of New England, 1975): 175-197.

Wholey, J. S., J. W. Scanlon, H. G. Duffy, J. S. Fukumoto, and L. M. Vogt, *Federal Evaluation Policy: Analyzing the Effects of Public Programs* (Washington, D.C.: Urban Institute, 1973).

Wildavsky, A., *The Politics of the Budgetary Process* (Boston: Little, Brown, 1974).

———, "The self-evaluating organization," *Public Administration Review* 32 (1972): 509-520.

Williams, W., "The capacity of social science organizations to perform large-scale evaluative research," *Public Policy Paper,* No. 2, Institute of Governmental Research, University of Washington, Seattle, 1971.

——— and J. W. Evans, "The politics of evaluation: the case of Head Start," *Annals of the American Academy of Political and Social Science* 385 (1969): 118-132.

Wilson, J. O. ,"Social experimentation and public-policy analysis," *Public Policy* 22 (1974): 15-37.

Wright, C. R., "Evaluating mass media campaigns," *International Social Science Bulletin* 7 (1955): 417-430.

NAME INDEX

SUBJECT INDEX